The Creativity Playbook

The Creativity Playbook

A Guide to our Creativity Debates

James S. Catterall

Professor Emeritus
UCLA Graduate School of Education
& Information Studies

September 2015

Centers for Research on Creativity

www.croc-lab.org

ISBN-13: 9781514311325

ISBN-10: 1514311321

DEDICATION

This book is dedicated to the artists in my family:

Ceramics Artist Rebecca Epps Catterall

Science Teacher and visual
curriculum specialist Lisa G. Catterall

Chemist Hannah Beth Catterall

Organizational Strategist
Grady James Catterall

and

Asta, Bogie, Daisy, and Bertha

Their work and lives attest to the power of creative thought and problem solving in crafting effective and rewarding lives.

The author thanks Rebecca Catterall and Gabriele Arenge for critical readings of the manuscript.

We thank the Panta Rhea Foundation for supporting this project.

Chompsky

ABOUT THIS BOOK

The Creativity Playbook examines nearly 30 frequently asked questions about human creativity and how it works. The Playbook also tackles less familiar questions about creativity in a down-to-earth style. The discussion features the work of well-known thinkers, e.g. Howard Gardner and Mihali Czikszentmihali, as well as artists who comment on their creative processes, e.g. cellist Yo-Yo Ma and the author himself.

The presentations are brief. We have tried to limit our comments to what is needed to grasp the essential points in each discussion and to avoid getting wrapped-up in technical or academic minutiae. References to extended work are provided. The book provides an Index to its key topics and personalities.

The book is written for teachers, parents, students, education policy leaders and legislators, academics doing research on creativity, and artists seeking to reflect in new ways on their own creative processes. The book is available in paperback and *Kindle* editions through Amazon. Place bulk orders through CRoC (www.croc-lab.org).

This book will help you to:

- Understand your thinking about creativity
- Win a few bets
- Know how to spell *Czikszentmihali*

ABOUT THE AUTHOR

James S. Catterall is Emeritus Professor of Education at the University of California at Los Angeles where he was a faculty member for 30 years and Chair of the Faculty for three elected terms. He is author of *Doing Well and Doing Good By Doing Art* (2009, I-Group Books) the most popular data-based analysis of the effects of learning in the arts ever published; Los Angeles, CA: I-Group Books. 5000 copies of this book are now in print.

Professor Catterall is also author of more than 100 research articles and scholarly book chapters including chapters on drama and transfer of learning in *Critical Links* (R. Deasy, Ed. (2002) Arts Education Partnership) and articles on arts partnerships and long term involvement in the arts in *Champions of Change* (E. Fiske, Ed. (1999): The MacArthur Foundation, The GE Fund.)

In 2011, Professor Catterall founded the Centers for Research on Creativity (CRoC) with Professor Anne Bamford of the University of the Arts, London, and Dr. Mark Runco, Torrance Professor of Creative Education and Gifted Studies at the University of Georgia.

ABOUT THE CENTERS FOR RESEARCH ON CREATIVITY (CRoC)

The Centers, based in Los Angeles and London, specialize in the measurement of creative growth and motivation of children and adolescents. Under the sponsorship of the Walt Disney Company, CRoC developed the *Next Generation Creativity Survey* (NGCS) for use in creativity-focused art and science programs. The NGCS is produced in pre- and post-forms that capture longitudinal change in skills, attitudes, and orientations. The survey gauges self-reports of creative behavior and scales actual creative products of test-takers. It includes measures of creative self-efficacy, collaboration, and empathy.

Leaders of art, music, graphic design, theatre, musical theatre, artscience, and school campus leadership programs participated in the design, development, and testing of the survey. As of 2015, about 3,500 students have taken the NGCS in 30 programs located in 10 U.S. states and Kenya. It is available in English, Spanish, and Swahili translations, along with an adaptation for ASD (autistic) elementary school children.

TABLE OF CONTENTS

Part I. Back to basics.

Part II. How Creativity Works

Part III. Creativity and our Schools

Part IV. Creativity and Human Development

Part V. Creativity in the Workplace

Part VI. Related Essays and Reports

PART I.
BACK TO BASICS.

CHAPTER 1

CREATIVITY DEBATES?? WHAT CREATIVITY DEBATES??

We all like the thought of creativity. And we surely tend to prefer more and not less of it around us and in ourselves, at least most of the time. So what's to debate?

Well, we might point out that some of us just like to argue. For example, a new aphorism in American culture goes something like this: if one candidate touts the need for a more creative citizenry, his opponent will find reasons to object and claim that math skills are the real problem. But there is more to debating creativity than the human urging to pick a fight.

Definition debates. At the center of important squabbles about human creativity are widespread beliefs that creativity is hard to measure and lacks an agreed-upon definition. Creativity is impossible to pin down with any precision. Thus one class of debates surrounding creativity is of the type, *if you can't define it and you can't tell how much of it you've got, then where could this conversation possibly lead?*

In some final analysis, creativity may have strong ties to gold and pornography. In response to M's question, "What do you know about gold?" James Bond replied, "I know it when I see it." And oddly in the same year (1964), U.S. Supreme Court Justice Potter Stewart wrote in a famous opinion that he'd be loath to define hardcore pornography, but, "I know it when I see it." Here we have to wonder which came first: *Goldfinger* or the Court's opinion?

Perhaps creativity is like that. Hard to define, but we know it when we see it. And, we know it when it's lacking. We might shy from arguments about who was more creative, Mozart or McCartney, Einstein or Martha Graham. Or about which of Neil Simon's plays was most inventive. Or whether Uncle Fred lost his creative drive when he bought his first TV. Tough to tell. But think a moment longer -- we love these sorts of arguments. It's just that we find them hard to settle. And nothing we could Google would help.

This debate surrounding creativity focuses on whether or not we can really detect it, or whether any two of us would agree on what we were seeing. Thus a reasonable response to a plea for more creative development in the schools might be, well, if we don't know what it is, how will we know it's happening? Or, if you want more creativity, how will you know when you're getting it? And was it worth the price you paid for it?

Debating what can we do about creativity. Disputes about creativity go way beyond confusions about what it is. Doing anything about creativity sparks controversy from the word "Go."

Our leaders have been urging more creativity on the part of American children and youth for several years. Creativity is occupying an ever more central place when presidents, governors, legislators and corporate chief executives hold forth on education and job training.

> *President Obama. In a recent State of the Union address, President Obama suggested that education policies should "grant schools flexibility to teach with creativity and passion; to stop teaching to the test." (Never mind that teaching creatively is one thing; teaching creative thinking and problem solving is another. We take up language imprecision surrounding creativity in Chapter 3.)*

> *IBM CEO Survey. A recent international survey of 1500 corporate CEOs reported that creativity is now the most important leadership quality for success in business, outweighing even integrity and global thinking.*

> *Nissan CEO. "Business begins with an idea. And as never before, its growth, stability, and ultimate success depend on innovation and a continuing flow of imaginative thought. The most urgent business of business is ideas."*

What we don't get from our leaders is guidance toward the next step: just how to go about teaching children to be creative, or how to change mere employees into *creatives*, as industry calls its innovators. For every 1,000 statements from on high about the need for creativity and innovation in our economy, we hear ... well not many, but a few reasonable plans for addressing that need. To be fair, our leaders are not typically in charge of getting actual things done – they articulate visions, the big pictures of the businesses' future, and leave action to others... sometimes!

Doing something in our case means developing and implementing policies that will improve conditions of creativity in industry or in the learning lives of our youngsters. We also debate, or should ponder, whether politicians and organizational leaders are really serious about what they ask for. Demanding something and not putting resources behind that demand ... that is not real demand, economists will assure you.

Creative human development debates. It's not just definitions and measurement or the practicalities of boosting creativity that get things stirred up. Psychologists and other academics (yes, it's our fault) may tussle harder about creativity than about other identified facets of cognitive and emotional development. The comparative uproar follows the fact that many fundamental psychological measures have gained consensus over the years, for example measures of intrinsic and extrinsic interest, self-efficacy, cognitive engagement, and attributions for success. Measures of creativity have not.

The tempests here have roots similar to those described above – measuring creativity has its limitations, has its proponents, and has its doubters among trained psychometricians (learning measurement specialists). But that's just a start. Psychologists argue about whether general creativity skills even exist, even though we may all know a

6-year old who is so generally creative that he needs two babysitters at once. We debate whether becoming creative in one area spills over to creative skills and motivation in others. As seen in other scientific conflicts, respected scholars reviewing the same mass of data and stacks of published articles sometimes hold differing opinions of what they are seeing.

The list of creativity debates is long. Readers will see in going through this guide that conflicts pop up everywhere. And end only in some cases. Is creativity a matter of intelligence? Is it a skill? A thinking disposition or habit?

We'll try to get through the issues with a sense of what holds up and what can't be justified when it comes to human creativity. Perhaps more important, you will know where and on what map to place a given statement or perspective on human imagination and ingenuity. You'll be a full participant in the debate.

And you can go around convincing others with your nuanced authority.

CHAPTER 2

SORTING OUT LANGUAGE: CREATIVITY SKILLS, CREATIVE THINKING, CREATIVE MOTIVATION, CREATIVE DISPOSITIONS, TEACHING CREATIVELY, TEACHING FOR CREATIVITY.

It might seem silly to quibble about language when considering creativity; but as it turns out, imprecision of language infects and clouds our creativity discussions. Why not trim this imprecision when there are much better things to be muddled about?

Creativity can mean different things to different people. Sometimes the use of the word simply raises hackles and horrifies the English teacher lurking in many of us. Let's sample what's out there.

Use your creativity when you build that sand castle.

This seems simple enough. Translation: Be creative! Decorate the castle in an unusual and pleasing way, or build into it some cool, novel functional shapes and connectors. *Your creativity* is your *capability and desire* to achieve something different, something you and others might like, something that might achieve a purpose in a new way.

Your creativity is evident!

Another easy one. Someone uses her creativity, or imaginative thinking, to achieve something, or to meet a challenge. Alice carved her pumpkin to resemble a flying saucer; the result looks creative because the result is unusual, at least for a jack-o-lantern. Its main value may be aesthetic. We wonder what made Alice think of that.

Do you teach musical creativity in your music program?

This can get a little prickly; so we need to dig in. The statement should mean: Do you teach students how to be creative as they engage the skills you're teaching? In other words, do your instructional routines produce creative musicians (or woodworkers, novelists, law-enforcers, what have you). This is a hugely important question to anyone interested in cultivating creative students and citizens – which is a main issue in this book.

Let's take this apart: If you teach someone to play the violin, the instruction is typically about technique; and learning to perform well involves exhaustive repetition and mimicking legendary musicians. It can take years to make a pleasing, musical sound on a violin, and creativity is not necessarily involved. The goals of early instrumental training may be little more than the advancement of technique and the issuance of quality sounds.

Contrast this to the sense of creativity illustrated here: *Are you teaching the young violinist to play with expression, or to evoke mood, or to symbolize emotion?* Adding original expressive qualities to an instrumental performance is a creative process, unless the expressions involved are confined to reproducing someone else's work, say from a recording or through parroting the instructor.

Yo-Yo Ma, the preeminent cellist, once demonstrated his thought and practice processes when learning a difficult piece. He began by figuring out how to play the written notes – complex double or triple stops (playing two or three strings at once), string crossings with the bow, finger reaches, and other sometimes painful contortions. He would do this slowly, measure by measure. This is not a creative process for the most part, but it is necessary first routine, as it would be for you or me. As Ma repeatedly played passages and the entire piece from start to finish, each rendition became not only more beautiful to listen to, but each drew on ways of playing that added specific expression. Achieving these expressions was a creative part of preparing and playing this musical work, and Ma pointed this out to his audience. He also demonstrated that he could play the same passage with highly varied emotional content and to very different overall effect.

Thus teaching expressive techniques is often about teaching *creativity* (i.e. teaching students to shape the tone and voice of their music in original ways to achieve their own desired expressions).

Music composition. Another example of teaching creativity is teaching music composition, in cases where students will compose original works. Students typically engage creative thinking and invention in producing new works of any scope.

Are you teaching creatively in your music program? This is yet another way the idea of creativity is used. Recall President Obama's urging education policies that freed teachers *to teach creatively* shown in Chapter 1. This question refers to how instruction is designed and carried out – and to the possibility that some instructional routines can be creative. Imagine that your way of teaching is simply not proving effective – and that inventing an alternative approach might pay off. Here is an example from personal experience: When learning to play cello, the student instinctively elevates the left elbow while navigating the fingerboard. This can cause problems for the learner with fingerings and with the vibrato. As a remedy, a teacher has the student hold a large orange under the left arm while playing. This seems creative. It appears to be novel. It works to temper the habit. Behold – creative instruction.

But whose creativity is involved? The orange device could be the oldest trick in the book. If the teacher thought-up this routine, the teacher was being creative (and was teaching creatively). If the teacher learned the technique from another teacher, she was using a creative technique, but not being personally creative. Perhaps the prior teacher was the creative one.

If this technique goes back to the 14th Century and had been passed down through the ages, perhaps no one in the chain was creative except some distant originator. But think about this: If a young teacher, never exposed to the orange trick, thought it up by himself, he was in fact being creative – creative even though the practice had been around for 600 years. This involves some detailed thinking, but you have to admit that the result is precise.

We'll say more about the *who's creative and who's not creative* idea in the next chapter: *Chapter 3. A unifying idea of creativity -- generating new and valuable ideas.*

More on creative teaching. Another example is fun. A cello instruction technique championed by a prominent teacher of cello teachers in the 1970s in San Francisco named Margaret Rowell, is the following: The learner lies, back-down on the floor, supporting the cello on top of her torso. Then she plays the cello from that position. This produces welcome effects. First, it sounds and feels nice (assuming you can play the thing decently to start with), because the musical vibrations of the cello invade the body. Second, this position allows the student to play using only the weight of the bow to push against the strings. This level of pressure is largely all you need or want when playing in a traditional position. The light feeling of the right hand on the bow takes a lot of tension out of the whole operation; and tension is a great enemy of high quality sound in the strings.

That's a clear example of teaching "creatively."

What about creative skills or creative capacity? The idea of creative skills is pervasive, but it's troublesome in light of some things we have learned about creativity.

The simplest way to put this concern is that creativity should not be thought of as a matter of skill. Hold on; you'll get more and more comfortable with this idea as you go further with this book. At very least, thinking creatively, or being creative, requires more than an identified or identifiable set of skills. Skills evoke images of techniques that once learned can be repeated with expected results -- on into the future. But creativity is not mainly about repetition; it's about doing and thinking new things and about approaching problems or challenges in new ways. Being generally creative means continuously engaging ways of thinking that are new or unconventional, welcoming possible new conceptions of things, flipping problems on their heads, and challenging knee-jerk assumptions about the difficulties or opportunities you face.

Thus any *skill* involved in creativity is not so much a cognitive processing skill but rather an inclination involved with how one approaches thought processing or problem solving, or how one goes about designing things to achieve desired purposes. In this formulation, creativity looks more like a habit of mind, or a disposition to address challenges in particular ways. Such dispositions may unfold without a shred of conscious thought; or they may result from monitoring our ways of thinking when trying to invent, design, or solve. We need to be conscious of the difference whenever we consider how to cultivate creativity in ourselves and in others.

Creative dispositions. And what are these dispositions? Think of a disposition as a tendency to behave or think in certain ways. Just to catalogue a few, they include being open to surprise in the search for solutions, to seeking-out and finding important problems in need of attention along the way, not jumping to hard judgments the moment a problem appears, willingness to take some risks, particularly the risk of proposing a wrong answer.

But visit the criticized notion of *creativity skills* once more. If being creative demands having some of the dispositional qualities just listed, the implications for cultivating creativity are enormous. To teach creativity, we are not challenged by problems of skill development in any typical sense, like learning to play tennis, to crochet, or to fly an airplane. We are challenged by fundamental issues of motivation to approach problems in certain ways, and orientation to those ways of thinking in the first place.

We take up the challenges of teaching creativity in Chapter 14 -- *Can Creativity be Taught? Means, Motive, and Opportunity.*

CHAPTER 3

THE UNIFYING IDEA OF CREATIVITY -- GENERATING NEW AND VALUABLE IDEAS.

D efinitions of creativity revolve around two core ideas. Successful creative processes lead to things that are *new* or *novel,* and that also have value. As examples, a creative *idea* is an *original* idea that can be put to some *use* – i.e. for a purpose that has value to someone. Guttenberg thought of his first printing press when he saw a simple wine grape press while traveling in Italy. The press operated when a threaded spindle was turned to force a wooden plunger into a slatted barrel of grapes. His idea for a printing press was an adaptation of this idea – an association or connection that led him to imagine a way of pressing ink-washed letter-shaped blocks onto a sheet of paper. This was a creative idea – a creative design, a creative product.

Guttenberg also created a novel *process* of printing at the same time – a *new* way of doing or achieving something that has value – the press was faster than previous printing processes and it's capacity to exert uniform pressure of letter carvings on paper render the printed products more uniform.

And of course, many creative adaptions followed over time – moveable type so that different print products would not require printing plates carved anew, placing printing negatives on the surface of a drum that could rotate and repeatedly press copies quickly, line-o-type machines that turned strokes on a typewriter-like keyboard into to letter type formed of molten lead that could be melted and re-formed into the next printing project (or the next day's newspaper) and of course injector and electrostatic machines used in modern printers that use no physical type faces at all. These major developments involved imagining automated printing processes that did not exist; and along the way, they undoubtedly drew on many creative steps needed to make the big idea work. The evolution of printing in grossly different ways happened in smaller steps through the accumulation of smaller ideas and inventions.

You get the idea anyway – new and valuable. Agreeing on this is helpful, and might win you an argument or two. But when we step beyond the novel and valuable in discussions of creative, significant disagreements emerge. They involve what we mean by new and by valuable. Or what qualifies as new or valuable.

What's new?

What should be meant by new? It turns out that after proclaiming the novel and valuable dictum, in one terminology or another, just what these terms mean is often unspecified. But at the same time, the meanings are implied by what the author or speaker includes through explanation and illustration.

New can mean lots of things. At one extreme, new might mean absolutely never before seen, truly unprecedented, or let's say *new on planet Earth*. This is a very restrictive definition, but it doesn't seem inconsistent with an idea, process, or object that truly did not exist before the inventor articulated or built the creation. Examples like the following fit this sort of new-ness, since somewhere along the way the first fully formed example appeared: Well, Guttenberg's printing press; the transistor; the fuel cell; the zipper; the bow and arrow. If you come up with something useful that no one has ever seen or heard of, you are dubbed creative, especially if you make a habit of this.

It's worth noting that many things that enter our lives through the workings of visionaries did not actually arrive as the invention of a single person imagining and executing the product. Profoundly important creations often build on earlier hopeful but not resolved ideas of predecessors. The story of the computer mouse is a good example. In the early 1970s, scientists at Xerox in Palo Alto toyed with the idea of some desktop shuttle controlling a computer cursor on a screen, along with a graphical user interface allowing some sort of switching, or clicking action on the shuttle to tell the computer what to do next (like clicking next!). At that time, personal computers were primitive and required typed instructions to engage in anything.

We've also heard the tale of Steve Jobs arranging for a tour of the Xerox Park labs – a privilege he obtained in exchange for allowing Xerox to purchase shares of Apple stock for a small fortune six years before the shining startup even went public. Now, that seems very creative in itself – getting yourself paid to see your competitor's secrets!

To keep the tale of the mouse brief, Jobs saw for the first time a clumsy rectangular wooden block of what would be considered an early computer mouse – one with a large steel ball suspended in ball bearings, that skipped errantly on trial surfaces, and whose ball mechanism gathered and gummed itself with dust and other desktop detritus beyond serviceability in a matter of an hour or two. This device was an improvement over an earlier design suspended on four roller-skate wheels. The estimated cost of manufacturing it?— $300.

Jobs was enchanted. Perhaps even more eye-popping to him during his visit to Xerox was his glimpse of the graphic interface – the idea of controlling a computer by directing a cursor to spots on a screen instead of typing commands.

Jobs came away with a vision for his own enterprise. He wanted a mouse for Apple Computers. A mouse that would work for a couple of years, and one that would cost only $15.00.

Apple Computer was on its way.

CHAPTER 4

NEW FOR WHOM? VALUABLE FOR WHOM

In this chapter, we pursue the critical ideas of novelty and value that lie at the heart of creativity.

Our early reviews of books on creativity began with Howard Gardner's volume, *Creating Minds.* (Some of our parents, mine anyway, began with Arthur Koestler's *Act of Creation,*[1] which gave sweeping and articulate attention to the important idea of *associative thinking.)* Gardner presents a group of extraordinarily creative people from diverse disciplines. His cast of characters includes Sigmund Freud, Albert Einstein, Pablo Picasso, Igor Stravinsky, T. S. Eliot,

---

1 Koestler, A. *Act of Creation.* London, U.K.: 1964.

Martha Graham, and Mahatma Gandhi. One purpose of Gardner's writing was to explore the diversity of "intelligences" that undergird creative thinking and innovation, or that support differences in the ways individuals learn. Interpersonal, mathematical, spatial, musical, linguistic, and kinesthetic understandings relate to the first six characters in the book, and Gandhi represents a seventh – interpersonal and political intelligences fit well. So a first lesson arises. Creativity manifests through many ways of understanding – Graham may see and express the world through movement, Stravinsky through music, Picasso through visual imagery. We attend to the importance of the creator's domains in creative behavior in a subsequent chapter.

But onward with the present theme. An implication of *Creating Minds* for us is the idea that extraordinary creativity is important, and perhaps the most important sort of creativity in our culture and society. Of course, this is naïve on our part. Gardner focused on these individuals precisely because of his own longstanding interest in extraordinary human behavior and accomplishment. And the lives of great, well-known creative individuals do inevitably interest readers.

Another leading book about creativity is Mihali Czikszentmihali's *Creativity: The Psychology of Optimal Experience.*[2] Like *Creating Minds*, this book reinforces the importance eminent creativity through interviews with visible *creatives* of the late 20th Century. The subject roster includes paleontologist Steven Jay Gould, economist Kenneth Boulding, actor Ed Asner, diva Kitty Carlisle Hart, sociologist David Reissman, biologist Jonas Salk, and *sitar* player and composer, Ravi Shankar. Czikszentmihali focuses on individu-

---

2 New York: Harper Collins: 1996.

als who imprinted symbolic domains in our culture – new ideas, philosophies, new songs – more generally, those who contributed visibly in the arts, sciences, business, and government.

As with Gardner in *Creating Minds*, Czikszentmihali's case studies might have reflected the author's interest in extraordinary creativity as a scholar of human development. But Mihali offers a revealing statement up front as he explains the essence of creativity.

> *"Creativity is some sort of mental activity, an insight that occurs inside the heads of some special people … If by creativity we mean an action that is new and valuable (mirroring our contention shown in Chapter 3), then we cannot simply accept a person's own account as the criterion for its existence. There is no way to know whether a thought is new except with reference to some standards, and there is no way to tell whether it is valuable until it passes social evaluation."*

So here we have ideas about creativity that align with an important definition presented in this volume – focusing on the new and the valuable. At the same time, these ideas are ultimately very constricting when it comes to either the broad spectrum of creative actions important to humankind or the fundamental importance of creativity in basic cognition and learning processes – creativity that helps account for how all humans progress from birth onward.

For the time being, we want to point out that, to some, creativity is mainly about extraordinary invention. While we benefit from great creativity, and we love new gadgets such as our I-*phones*, *George Foreman* grills, and intercontinental ballistic missiles, ordinary creativity has vast importance that must be recognized if we want to pursue a national agenda of creative development that touches all and benefits society broadly.

In fact, many observe that creativity lies at the cornerstone of thinking and problem solving at the most basic levels. Instead of applying criteria of greatness and prestige or disciplinary importance when we sort out questions of value and novelty, in reality these criteria have nothing much to do with whether or not the objects in our attention are creative, to wit:

An idea or envisioned object should be considered NOVEL or NEW if it is NOVEL OR NEW to the creator. Period. The 11 year old who invents an unfamiliar (novel) idea as part of attempting to solve a science problem is in fact being creative. 1) The idea is new to the inventor, and 2) it's almost certain to have value. The idea may contribute to a successful solution; and just as important, the idea may serve to point out where solutions do not reside – this is just as helpful as a positive hint, really.

So something of a mantra follows this book: It's new if it's new to you; and it's valuable if it's valuable to you. Gradations of novelty and value are other matters; they do not factor into whether something is creative or not. We could allow that such gradations might figure into how creative we might judge an idea or invention to be (i.e. how novel or how valuable), but that's really another story. Notice how Csikszentmihalyi picks on the little inventors and innovators among us by inserting the issue of privileged knowledge.

> *"Creativity is some sort of mental activity, an insight that occurs inside the heads of some special people ... If by creativity we mean an action that is new and valuable ...,*

then we cannot simply accept a person's own account as the criterion for its existence. There is no way to know whether a thought is new except with <u>reference to some standards</u>, and there is no way to tell whether it is valuable until it passes <u>social evaluation</u>." (Emphasis added.)

The problem with this formulation is that an idea or invention is not creative unless some class of judges anoints it with special status in a field. We would say that this may establish a certain type of creative act or invention, but this is not a required quality of things in order for them to be called creative. I prefer to let Csikszentmihalyi play in playgrounds of his own choosing and leave others to call small children creative when they hatch ideas and inventions that are simply new to them and valuable to them, Csikszentmihalyi appraisals not withstanding.

CHAPTER 5

ARE CREATIVITY AND INNOVATION THE SAME THING? NO!

Creativity and Innovation are not the same thing, at least not in modern American Usage. Innovation is typcally used to mark the creation of a new device or an improvement on an existing processs that <u>contributes value in a commercial context</u> ... for example, this water hoop is the first one we've seen where half of it floats and half of it sinks and can be used in a new game ... or the double switch on this electric razor allows the device to be used to cut toe nails if that is what you'd like to do with it. This lawnmower is innovative because it turns grass clippings into fertilizer with the addition of phosphrous in a special hopper.

A common attribute of things we call innovations is the addition of some feature or design that helps a product work better ... adding a plastic bottle holder to the frame of a bicycle; think on this for a movent. The holder sounds like a creative product, an invention. The idea and implementation of installing such a holder sounds like an innovation.

These distictions are not particularly important. We do detect that in conversations about creativity, discussions of innovations in fact aim at the productive economy more than not; and many outcries for a more creative workforce are driven by desires on the part of business leaders and polititians for more innovative, competitive products that will create markets, expand market shares, bring advantages to (typically OUR) markets in the cause of the Gross National Product. Somehow, the clever drawing in elementary school, the robotic monopoly money changer, and the tile bridge over the school walkway all sport *creative* rather than *innovative* as descriptors.

Don't be surprised if you naturally turn to innovation when you speak of creative things in the economic domain and creative when you speak of creative things in the worlds of art, education, and aesthetics.

PART II.
HOW CREATIVITY WORKS

CREATIVITY AND THE LEARNING PROCESS – WHAT'S NEW TO YOU, AND WHAT'S VALUABLE TO YOU WHEN SEEKING UNDERSTANDING AND SOLVING PROBLEMS.

When we try to solve a problem, whether it's a jammed bicycle hub or a science question in fourth grade, we often hatch ideas about possible solutions. These are our own ideas, assuming we are working by ourselves. That's enough to qualify for the *novel* part of creativity's definition. And the ideas typically have value – they pay off and guide us to problem solutions, or they lead us to dead-ends that show us where not to look for helpful guidance. This is not blockbuster or extraordinary creativity in action. But it's creativity that proves extraordinarily important.

So instead of laboring about noteworthy inventions or ideas truly never before seen, we focus in the learning sciences on personal, or ordinary creativity -- or "*little c*" creativity as James Kaufman calls this. It may be ordinary, but it is very important in our lives and near infinitely more prevalent than creative acts that turn others' heads or earn their inventors fortunes.

Try an experiment or two with yourself on this. As you are driving, or walking, or perhaps even sitting in front of a television program, put a little effort into meta-cognition. That is, give a little thought to the images and ideas that role through you mind at the same time you are doing these things. You may be amazed by the pace and variety of the "slide show" this produces.

The images result from spontaneous connecting sponsored by your brain as you are stimulated by most anything. The brain is an overachiever on this count – it just takes hold and connects.

Then try the experiment another way. Try to concentrate on a single problem or issue as you go about your driving, walking, or TV watching. What you are likely to find is that your brain butts in and interferes with your work, sometimes helpfully but more often on its and not your agenda.

We have called this process cognitive distraction, which affects everyone. It's probable that through some conscious regulation, one could diminish the distracting nature, and enhance the productive nature of such distractions. This is certainly a prospect of great potential interest to any educator or learner wishing to boost capacity to concentrate. And it relates to what our teachers probably referred to as mental discipline.

Generating ideas at a fast clip may be distracting, but it's indicative of a healthy, active mind, one equipped to approach problems creatively, to generate possible solutions, and leave you with good choices when it comes time to act.

CHAPTER 7

ASSOCIATIVE AND DIVERGENT THINKING: KEY CONTRIBUTORS TO CONNECTION MAKING AND HATCHING NEW IDEAS.

Many creative thoughts and designs result from connecting one idea or image to another. Einstein wrote of combining and manipulating images in reaching his *unified theory*. The unexpected juxtaposition of ideas or images is a major source of humor, according to psychologists – humorous ideas are generally thought to be creative (novel, yes; and to some as valuable as the Swiffer!)

When we read or hear a word, or an idea, we instantaneously and reflexively seek and find associations with that idea. These are processed broadly throughout the brain's cortex. The results of some associations surface to our conscious minds, for reasons only partly understood. Some associations seem natural and obvious, some are obscure though understood by their adopters, some are outrageous.

It's probable that domain knowledge has something to do with the types and numbers of associations we make with specific ideas. When a non-chemist hears "molar weight," the associations made are limited and probably not related to chemistry – but perhaps to teeth. The chemist who works with the concept has many places to go to connect the idea.

This suggests a relationship that has not been tested. This is that individuals with vast general knowledge may be positioned to be highly creative in a general sense. They have lots of raw material for connection making.

As for speed in connection making, the most relevant idea from brain studies is that neurological circuits get more efficient with regular use and grow less efficient with lack of use. Someone used to seeking associations actively probably has an advantage over someone who is non-attentive to this or lacking experiences where active connection seeking is required. Nonetheless, the brain will seek out associations regardless of individual motivation so many circuits will work well no matter how we approach association-making.

CHAPTER 8

AN EVERYMAN'S GUIDE TO THE NEUROSCIENCE OF ASSOCIATIVE THINKING.

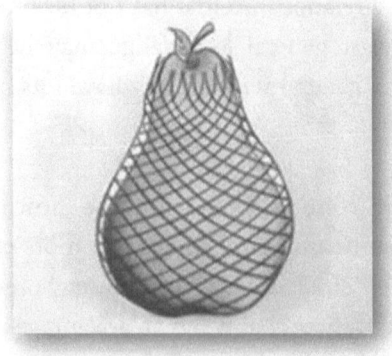

You must be kidding! A pear??!!

Neuroscientist/psychiatrist Nancy Andreason M.D. Ph.D.[3] characterizes the neural substrates (location and dynamics of brain activity) of creative thinking as the making of associations between previously unassociated ideas. In this chapter, we take the principles of associative thinking to the level of neuroanatomy and neuro-function. This glimpse has implications for how we can help individuals to be more creative.

---

3 *The Creating Brain: The Neuroscience of Genius.* Washington DC: The Dana Press, 2005

To start, think of a pear with a protective Styrofoam net at a posh market, and this net as a web of possible cortical connections. Remember the brain's cortex is the many-folded gray layer of cells surrounding the interior regions of the brain – or on the surface of what we call the brain. While there are many pathways of neuronal connection within the brain, it is pathways within and across the cortex that account for a vast majority of connections we would call "associations." When we connect a duck's web foot to a propeller blade (why not?), it is the "image" or "concept" or "thought of the propeller "located somewhere in the brain's cortex that becomes "connected" with the duck's foot; the two then are thought-of, more or less, as a single associated thought (they both impel objects through a medium).

Whatever you had in mind for the duck's foot can now incorporate the propeller blade and become something else in your imagination, or something similar in shape with different purpose, and so on. Perhaps something never seen before, something capable of accomplishing something never before accomplished.

Efficiency. Two principles related to associative thinking come to mind as we approach this subject. One is a notion of efficiency. The brain generally gets more efficient at what it does by repeated actions or similar actions. This points to a learning process, one that can be seen in images of the brain learning in action. When an expert pianist struggles with a very difficult new piece, fMRI images of the brain taken while the pianist works on the composition are typically well lighted, showing many parts of the brain engaged in the piano performance. After weeks of practice on the same work and the achievement of fluid competency, the same brain shows little indication of active effort to play the piece expertly. The brain has become efficient at playing the piece; the motor pathways become more familiarly traveled, and the brain does not have to work as hard to achieve the work. The resulting fMRI scan shows very little illumination.

Connectible content. Let's risk a small redundancy. We make an assumption when we think of associative thinking that has demonstrated little by way of proof, but almost certainly will hold up as experiments in associative thinking move forward. This is that the more "content" knowledge an individual can be said to possess, the more likely are associations likely to succeed in being realized in this sort of thinking process. A hydrologist casting about for ways to connect pipes of diverse metals needs some knowledge of relevant metallurgy to boost chances of achieving a productive connection. Or as we sometimes say, we need to know some chemistry to be a creative chemist.

CHAPTER 9

ASSOCIATIVE THINKING LIES AT THE CENTER OF CREATIVE COLLABORATION.

More Fruit??!!

The neurological model we build through Chapters 8 and 9 illustrates vividly how key aspects of collaborative creation and design work. For many thinking purposes, two heads are better than one.

In this chapter, we show an image of not one pear in its protective net, but two apples in their respective nets "collaborating." The apples are brains and the nets depict associative connections.

When the left apple expresses an idea, it connects this idea or expression to another idea – one of about 100 million possible primary connections even though only 50 or so are modeled in the sketch.

AND then the right-hand apple makes a connection to its collaborator's first idea as well; this precipitates a pattern of first-round connections across both apples or brains that number roughly one trillion.

We have conducted numerous small experiments in graduate classes, college classes, and school classes related to this and found good evidence for the advantages of collaboration, especially among subjects who find association-making challenging on their own.

In these experiments we ask the class to individually come up with uses for an object, in one version a one inch wide flat strip of metal bent into a rectangular u-shaped object about one foot on each of three sides. In five minutes, the most uses listed is typically about fifteen; the fewest four or five. Knowing these results, the instructor then pairs students with particular attention to coupling the lowest performers. Given a second opportunity to invent uses, this time for a clear Plexiglas triangle about six inches on a side and one inch thick, the low performers come up with about 12 to 15 uses. This is quite an improvement. It seems to result from 1) the power of two brains bouncing ideas off of each other and achieving associations, and 2) the increased familiarity with a second go at the "uses" task.

Some of the uses are of course seen as more creative than others. The u-shaped piece of metal is immediately seen as a croquet wicket or a dysfunctional corral for midget cattle. One school principal thought the object could serve as a pen at the back of a classroom to confine misbehaving students, well one misbehaving student anyway.

If you conduct such an experiment yourself (it's good fun!), you can take the discussion in interesting directions when it comes to the nature of creativity.

Imagine the same experiment going on hundreds of times simultaneously in different locales. The same uses, even obscure ones, are likely to pop up in multiple places.

Are these "uses" creative? According to the principles we avow, yes they are. They were originated by the individuals involved, and they have value – at least as small successes in the experiment. Or they may be aesthetic, or funny. So they are novel and they have value, at least to the individual and probably to the group when a discussion unfolds.

CHAPTER 10

IS THERE SUCH THING AS GENERAL CREATIVITY? IS MOST CREATIVE THINKING AND PROBLEM SOLVING DOMAIN-SPECIFIC?

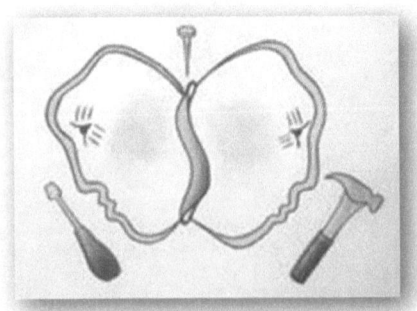

G eneral creativity refers to creative capacity or creative dispositions that an individual may apply in diverse problem situations – such as keeping a theatre set from falling over, or helping solve a neighborhood pollution issue. Some people seem rather consistently creative in many situations. Domain-specific creativity refers to acts of creativity that focus on one type of problem, or in one discipline. A creative biologist may not be creative in non-biological pursuits. In this chapter, we propose that both types of creativity exist and are important.

This discussion is vital. It bears on whether or not boosting creative capacity and motivation in one domain (e.g. through a middle school art class) can boost creative capacity and motivation more generally. Research evidence supports this idea.

Recall in our discussion of Czikszentmihali when he stated that to be considered creative, one needed to be regarded by domain peers, i.e., experts with specialized knowledge, as creative in the respective field. In other words, if you were to be thought a creative ham radio operator, you would first have to be considered expert with the radio, and then other experts would be valid judges of your creativity in that field. That is domain-specific creativity. Czikszentmihali's definition of creative implies that creativity is not likely to be general, or that it may be general only when one has deep specialized knowledge in multiple specialties.

If you do demonstrate abilities and motivation to come up with new and valuable ideas across a wide spectrum of domains, you are considered to be generally creative.

An observation in one of our experiments suggests that some people tend to possess general creativity to some degree. This is because the ability to associate or connect ideas does in fact seem to vary systematically across individuals and across trials at generating ideas – recall the apple and pear model classroom experiments involving the iron "u-shaped" artifact and the Plexiglas triangle.

CHAPTER 11

CONTEXT MATTERS: MANY IF NOT MOST CREATIVE INSIGHTS AND INVENTIONS HAVE ROOTS IN THE CONTEXTS OF THEIR INVENTORS. MANY CREATIVE ACTS AND PRODUCTS MATTER MAINLY TO AN INVENTOR'S PEERS.

Despite acceptance that general creativity exists, we see that the context of the creator regularly influences creative processes. Creatives often work amidst peers who strive to achieve in a common context. Or in a milieu that influences their creative products. For example, Shakespeare's creativity ties directly to the 16th Century world of his Elizabethan London. The social and legal snarls that envelope his characters are those of his times, despite their links to the durable human condition.

And in the case of domain creatives, say in theoretical physics or gastroenterology, their creative work inhabits the technical and cultural environs of their specialties, and the scientific technologies of the present day.

It may sound simplistic, but the context issue bears hard on the association of ideas. Association of one idea with a thought may be exceedingly clever – funny, useful, valuable. The same association of the same ideas could result in nothing creative if it was drawn into a non-resonating context.

Specific genres of humor work this way. Humor involving clowns may work well in the circus, or with children of certain ages, or when it involves cars that bump into each other. Absent their contexts, the jokes may fall flat.

But we do recognize this. Creative writers make careers within contexts in many cases. They do their associating of ideas within circles of subjects, cultures, and geographies. In doing so, we see elements of context as important to creative behavior and motivation.

BEYOND MAKING ASSOCIATIONS; INSIGHTS INTO CREATIVE PROCESSES IN THE BRAIN REVEAL PROACTIVE AND INHIBITING ACTIONS IN THE FRONTAL REGIONS. IMAGING JAZZ MUSICIANS WHILE THEY IMPROVISE PROVIDES A CLASSIC CASE.

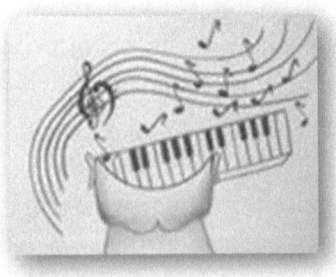

We are rightfully curious how our brains do things. In the case of creative thinking, there is sense of brain function that poses questions about what the brain inhibits as well as what it does to allow or impel certain functions. Creativity turns out to be a combination of assertive action and relaxed inhibition on the part of the brain. We discuss a recent brain-imaging study of jazz improvisation by Charles Limb M.D. at Johns Hopkins University to make these points. Limb studied jazz musicians playing routinized pieces (together, often in harmony) as well as during improvisational passages.

He was interested in how the brain functioned as musicians improvised as well as when they played familiar, organized songs.

Limb had to improvise (invent, really) to engage in this experiment. He wanted to use an fMRI scanner to map activations in the brain while the musicians played. FMRI scanners generate tremendous amounts of magnetic energy while they function – enough so that any metal part inside the scanner core would be very likely to be ejected at the speed of a bullet if subjected to the magnetic force. To circumvent this problem, Limb built a keyboard involving no metal parts for the pianist in his scanner.

The results were robust. The pianist played while listening to his fellow musicians through headphones. They could improvise this way, or play more standard, planned works. The improvisation condition revealed a brain that had diminished functioning in the limbic, or evaluative regions. (The Limbic system is a constellation of brain structures that acts together to evaluate ideas. It includes the amygdala, the hippocampus, the hypothalmus, and nearby areas surrounding the thalmus.) The brain essentially turned itself loose to improvise. While playing standard, planned songs, the limbic system engaged in much evaluating and editing, presumably in order to "get things right."

We can imagine many scenarios where demands for order, tolerance of disorder, and desires for disorder are transmitted through the brain – and that the resulting regulation and non-regulatory neural processes probably bear resemblances to what Limb found in his study.

CHAPTER 13

SORTING OUT IMAGES OF TECHNOLOGY: CREATIVITY AND INVENTING; CREATIVITY IN USING INVENTIONS; USING TECHNOLOGY TO INVENT. KEEPING THINGS STRAIGHT.

C reativity conjures images of technological inventions these days. Google's driverless car, commercial video streaming, robotic surgery devices, powerful statistical analysis software, smart phones, and industry robotics. It's easy to think that creativity in technology refers mainly to inventing and innovating with these developments. Fair enough.

When we conjure images of our children easing their lives into an adulthood rife with unprecedented technologies arriving like clockwork, it's natural to imagine the roles of your children. This vision of course is to join the ranks of technologists inventing important new devices.

Being inventive at the level of new commercial devices is a very small piece of the action when it comes to human creativity. Most human work related to technologies will be in using existing technologies to accomplish and build. Let's try some conservative numbers.

Who Works on What Worldwide? (guestimates)

- People who use smartphone apps during creating/ inventing, broadly construed: 20,000,000.
- People who use the pool of modern technology worldwide to build, create, and invent other things: 200,000,000.
- People who write computer code: 250,000.
- People who invent apps for phones and computers: 50,000 (1.5 million apps exist for each of the Iphone and android systems as of 2015)
- People who invent smart phone technologies: 20,000

The numbers of creatives working to invent and improve technologies themselves is much, much smaller than the numbers of us who use recent and emerging technologies to accomplish additional things. For example, for every one person who plays a role in *designing* and inventing computer hardware and software, there are millions of people who use computers for a great range of things, including creative work.

What does this assessment mean when we think of helping large numbers of children, youth, and adults to be more creative through such experiences as school and after-school programs? Should we focus on inventing technological blockbusters, or on the creative use of existing technologies in order to provide value? This latter might be called technology literacy and when it comes to the larger picture of technology-based creativity in our society. The lion's share of the action resides here and not in the quest for blockbuster devices. An example is using the blockbuster GPS technology to design a system for hailing taxicabs and blockbuster financial software to pay for your ride. Think *Uber* and *Lyft*.

PART III.
CREATIVITY AND OUR SCHOOLS

CHAPTER 14

CAN CREATIVE THINKING CAPACITY BE TAUGHT? ARE SOME CREATORS BORN AND NOT MADE?

These questions bear the hallmarks of core debates in learning and development. They bring to mind a similar and central controversy surrounding human intelligence – whether or not intelligence is something we are born with and whether or not it can be boosted or shaped by learning experiences.

Research and practical experience suggest that creativity can be something of a stable trait. Many studies also indicate that encouraging children and youth to engage in creative experiences, and providing time for creative pursuits, can increase tendencies to approach future problems and challenges creatively.

As with *intelligence*, these questions involve definition: what we mean by *creativity*. Perhaps not surprisingly, creative behavior may depend as much or more on motivation than on capacity or talent.

If the scales on the Next Generation Creativity Survey bear some validity, students do gain creativity skills and motivation in high quality programs – programs in theatre, musical theatre, social problem solving, graphic design, and integrated arts and science. Their creativity scores increase over the course of instructional programs. Their beliefs in their own creativity grow, and the views of trained scorers often agree that the creative qualities of student ideas and products also increase.

DeHaan[4] reviewed literature related to teaching creative skills and motivation, in the context of science education. He describes qualities of programs that associate with significant effect sizes on the measured creativity of subjects, as follows:

- Model creativity. Instructors must demonstrate creative approaches to problem solving and surface key features of those processes. The classroom discussion must explicitly involve the fact that creativity is a goal and is a key subject of attention.
- Repeatedly encourage idea generation – by individuals and by groups.
- Cross-fertilize ideas. Bring multiple disciplines to bear on ideas.
- Build self-efficacy beliefs. Students must be encouraged to believe that they can create and placed in situations where they can see this happening.

---

4 R. L. DeHaan (2009). *Teaching Creativity and Inventive Problem Solving in Science Education.* CBE Life Science Education, Fall, 8(3): 172-181.

- Constantly question assumptions. Make questioning a routine part of classroom exchanges.
- Imagine other viewpoints. In the divergent thinking phases of approaching problems, encourage generation of multiple viewpoints on problems and possible solutions.

Chapter 26 presents a sample evaluation of a societal art-science problem-solving program from 2014. You will notice attention to DeHaan's ideas in how we talk about and appraise the conduct of this idea laboratory program.

Means, Motive, and Opportunity

Another perspective on teaching for creativity comes through the lenses of "means, motive, and opportunity." These are the legendary conditions under which one can fall under suspicion of homicide. Well, it turns out the means, motive, and opportunity are handy to identify in creativity-focused programs for children and youth.

Means. If children are to be creative, they need the means to be so. This refers to the materials and tools of creation. Perhaps it's a brain, a body, some relevant knowledge, and a word processor if you are a writer. Or construction paper, scissors, staplers, and marbles if you are devising a marble roller coaster. Teaching for creativity often begins with gaining facility with the materials and tools of creation —how to fashion and fasten materials to create the designs you have in mind.

Motive. Beyond materials for creating, you need motivation to do something with the materials and tools. This is not usually a problem in the context of children involved in education for creativity.

Too much eagerness and motivation is a more likely condition. Place a table of bits, some glue, some string, and elastic bands in front of a child and you need do no more to put the whole class in motion toward some end – just ask the kids what they are building.

Opportunity. A creative workshop for children implies opportunity to get to work. Opportunity becomes a key issue when creativity is a desired but not necessary part of the teaching and learning agenda. By this we mean teaching designs must allow for creative time, idea-generation, feedback, trials, re-trials, and demonstrations if teaching for creativity is important. The science classroom is a good example. The work of science is investigatory and problem-solving focused. The learning of science in school may or may not maintain this focus. And it will only have this focus if the teaching plan provides opportunities for its exercise.

CHAPTER 15

CAN INDIVIDUAL CREATIVE PERFORMANCE BE MEASURED? YES.

Whether or not creativity can be measured is sometimes the first question tossed at us creativity researchers by educators, parents, and scholars. The implied concern is that creativity can't be measured and it thus may not be worth discussion or research. If we compare the number of active creativity researchers (very small) to the membership numbers of the American Psychological Association (very large), this concern is worth considering.

We offer a case that creative abilities, creative behavior, creative products, and creative motivation do submit to measurement. Using standards of test reliability and test validity, meaningful measures of creative thinking and creative products are available, and efforts are underway, including those at CRoC, to improve creativity assessments. We demonstrate this in the Chapter 26 case study of the idea laboratories.

Our leading contemporary creativity test is the *Next Generation Creativity Survey* developed by the *Centers for Research on Creativity* for the Walt Disney Company in 2012.

This test uses several traditional self-report scales to gather students' self-ratings on creative capacity and behavior. It also uses less traditional scales of collaboration skills and orientations, and a less frequently used scale of empathic orientations. And the test has adult scorer ratings of actual creative tasks undertaken by those tested. Here is an outline:

Student self-reports of their creativity.
Our self-report measures include the following:

- Creative Motivation – eagerness to be creative; choosing creative actions
- Creative Problem Solving – approaching problems in creative ways; trying alternative solutions, experimenting, taking risks of making mistakes and errors
- Creative Self-efficacy Beliefs – believing one has high creative skills
- Originality – believing one generates novel or new ideas
- Collaboration Attitudes and Skills – enjoying collaboration; personal tendencies to be collaborative
- Creative Fluency – able to generate many ideas
- Empathy – understanding and responding to the feelings of others

Demonstrated creativity growth.

We rate students' creative products on the *NGCS* in the following six areas:

- Demonstrated Creative Fluency: Generating more rather than fewer ideas
- Proportion (%) of Expressed Ideas Rated as Original. This item focused on student responses to our, "How would the world be different if ...?" questions[5]
- Ideas Rated as Valuable: Same item focus. Generating useful or aesthetic ideas to the "What if..." prompts
- Ideas Rated Original: Generating new or novel ideas across open items
- Drawing is Creative: Judges rating of student self-portrait

After testing 3500 subjects, we are finding that these scales and ratings do a good job of differentiating between students highly versus less motivated and fluent when it comes to creating ideas and products that are novel and valuable – the point of the test in the first place.

---

5   An example of this survey item is the prompt: "How would your life be different if all animals spoke fluent English and Spanish?" Students have four minutes to inventory their speculations on this question.

CHAPTER 16

IS CREATIVITY BASICALLY A MATTER OF INTELLIGENCE? NO.

Psychologist Robert Sternberg wrestled with data concerning this question over some years and concluded that more intelligent individuals are not necessarily or even typically more creative. He finds that highly creative people typically score somewhere in the vast mid-range (80-90 percent) of the intelligence distribution, and that extreme intelligence doesn't correlate with high creativity. He also found that highly creative people are not likely to hail from the ranks of very low measured intelligence. Of course, exceptions abound.

But there is good reason to keep watchful here. Different scholars define intelligence and creativity in different ways. Any study suggesting a particular relationship between intelligence and creativity can easily differ from other studies because they are not addressing the same constructs. Having said this, there are not many recent studies out there on this topic.

CHAPTER 17

CAN WE EVALUATE CLASSES AND WORKSHOPS FOR THEIR ABILITY TO NURTURE CREATIVITY? YES.

If we can satisfy ourselves on our ability to measure individual creative thinking ability, or ability to craft creative things, or ability to solve problems in a creative way (we demonstrated this in Chapter 15), we have a good start on this question. A *good* individual creativity measure can support a *very* good group creativity measure because group measures typically have less measurement error than individual measures (for one reason, the tendency of individuals to have good and bad days averages out). By "group" measure, we mean a scale that captures how well a group performs on a measure, say after participating in a class. This group principle goes as well for a 5th grade robot-making workshop as it does for a Media Lab design workshop at M.I.T. If we can assess participants entering a program on one or more dimensions of creative behavior, and assess the participants again after participation in the program, we may be able to support contentions that the program boosted creativity. Well-designed comparison group research can work too. We must not forget that this work should proceed from reasonable theories about why a particular program might boost the creative skills we are measuring. And that observing programs in action is a good way to capture just how and why they lead to what results.

When we engage in evaluations of creativity-focused programs, we use both measures of individual gains in creativity, and observations of the classes in action to generate hypotheses and rationales for why the program achieved what it did. Or why it succeeded more in some sorts of creativity measures than others.

CHAPTER 18

ARTS EDUCATION IN THE SCHOOLS AND CREATIVE DEVELOPMENT – A PLAYER AMONG PLAYERS.

T he visual and performing arts offer many opportunities for youngsters (and those of any age) to exercise creativity – to create new and novel things that are valuable to someone. The arts contribute to some schools' overarching identities, where they think of themselves as hotbeds of creativity and creative development. But many things that go on in schools the name of art do not involve much or any creativity to speak of; and much that goes on in school in non-art disciplines can involve more creativity than inside or outside observers would expect.

A music program that focuses exclusively on instrumental performance skills may produce violinists and trumpet players who play skillfully and beautifully – but who have never exercised a creative thought in reaching their heights of talent. The visual arts class may turn students loose to create freely. Or it may push students toward replicating other works or drawing natural scenes exactly as the eye perceives these, and where the slip of a brush is an error. Valuable, probably. New or novel, probably not.

And the high school chemistry class that we all remember to have occupied us with endless memorization of elements, compounds, and synthesizing equations can in fact focus on creative activity. Students may identify substances with combinations of trials and reasoning, a common practice in industrial quality control; or devise a color that no one has ever seen for a piece of jewelry.

If we want to boost creative skills and dispositions through the schools, the arts of course should play a role. But there are extensive opportunities for creative work across the disciplines that should be seized.

CHAPTER 19

THE WORK OF SCIENCE AS PLAY AND INVENTION; HOW ABOUT THE WORLD OF SCIENCE EDUCATION?

S cientists tell us that their work is mainly play. That is, they play with materials, processes, and ideas in order to discover new materials, processes, and ideas. Let's push this a little bit and say that science is inquiry and problem focused; and that processes of inquiry and problem exploring typically involve creative actions.

We include among these: brainstorming ideas, formulating guesses and hypotheses, testing ideas and hypotheses, revising thinking and reaching new hypotheses, confirming solutions, implementing results (perhaps). The scientist goes through, sometimes alone but more often as part of a local or dispersed team, processes of divergent and exploratory thinking followed by convergent thinking as signs begin to point to solutions, assuming success toward solving the problem(s) is at hand.

Some school and university science education programs encourage students to behave like scientists – where students play with ideas. Some school science is more about memorizing names, dates, inventions, connections, and equations. What was your experience like?

There is great room in science – biology, chemistry, physics, environmental/life science, computer science – for creative pursuits in the service of learning. And opportunities for the deep sorts of learning that can come from solving problems through creative thinking. A difficulty faced by teachers wanting to imbue their science classes with hands-on creative experiences is that teaching science effectively is often viewed as a matter of curricular coverage – getting the names, inventions, and formula's straight. Or as a matter of following prescriptive guides to experiments. Creative tangents will interfere with progressions to the end of the book by the end of the school year.

The Common Core and science. We wonder whether new tests in science aligned with the Common Core will call for a different kind of science teaching and learning, and whether the standards and tests used across the country will be in alignment on this. It's a bold statement to say that you are teaching science based on creative problem solving; it's a curricular challenge; and it's an unprecedented standardized test that will tell you whether you have actually succeeded in this.

PART IV.
CREATIVITY AND
HUMAN DEVELOPMENT

CHAPTER 20

CREATIVITY AND SELF-EFFICACY.

C RoC's work with learning in and through the arts supports an important contention. This is that when students become competent through a sustained artistic (visual or performance) learning experience, they become more self-confident and think of themselves as more skilled or efficacious in the discipline. In addition, there is evidence that increasing artistic self-efficacy beliefs can contribute to increased self-efficacy beliefs more generally. Some of this evidence comes through observing student behavior outside of the arts classes and linking this with in-class developments. The mechanisms are interesting -- self-reflection along with peer and teacher feedback regarding students' skills seem to be involved.

We use an adaptation of the traditional motivation-related measure of self-efficacy in our *Next Generation Creativity Survey*. This operates through self-report questions such as "I find it easy to come up with lots of ideas when I face a problem." We call the resulting scale *creative self-efficacy beliefs*.

We find in modal creativity focused program evaluations that half or more of the participants gain significantly on this scale. And in some programs, the students gain significantly overall on their group's creative self-efficacy score.

Examples of this can be seen in Chapter 26, where we show illustrative results based on our survey.

CHAPTER 21

CREATIVITY, EMPATHY, AND COLLABORATION

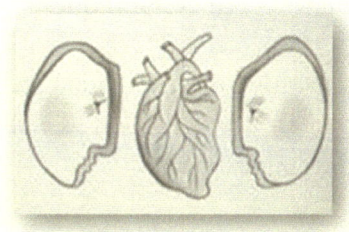

We set out to devise a new and better creativity tests in the fall of 2011. When we met with the heads of diverse creativity-focused programs to discuss what it was they hoped to teach through their efforts, we repeatedly heard some ideas that we did not expect. One was collaboration skills; a second with empathy orientations.

Empathy had been on our minds for years. When asked what it is we want most in the preparations and toolkits of young adults, our answer was ready: we'd like our citizens to have empathy for fellow human beings – to see the world through the eyes of others and to have consideration for their circumstances and problems. The focus on empathy we found in the programs we explored surprised – and pleased – us. We eventually built an empathy assessment into our test.

It turns out that empathy was a good lead-in to the question of collaboration orientations and skills, something also on the minds of our program respondents. We have been involved in a score or more of creativity-focused programs in the past three years. Every one of these programs uses a collaborative work model at its center. We can't say that it's the special power of collaboration serving creative purposes that drives this, or that it is the recent rise in popularity of collaborative project based learning more generally that we confronted.

Either way, collaboration seems a natural when students can learn from each other and put the power of associating brains together in service of their assignments and personal quests.

High levels of empathy and collaboration go hand in hand in our data. Caring about others probably leads to better working relations when people are joined in group tasks.

The diverse creativity-focused programs CRoC works with all seem interested in their programs' effects on empathy, as we said above. This is consistent with recent observations that learning in the arts can contribute positively to individual empathetic dispositions. One theoretical foundation for the connection ties to processes of detecting feeling or intention in artistically presented figures. Another has to do with practices of collaboration and ensemble work in the arts, which benefit from empathy.

CRoC's early work with an empathy scale in the Next Generation Creativity Survey suggests such connections.

See Chapter 29 for a detailed report of a CRoC study of the neuroscience of empathy and art. [6]

---

6   Catterall, J. S. *A neuroscience of empathy and art: aligning brain imaging and behavioral evidence.* www.croc-lab.org. (2011).

CHAPTER 22

RECAPPING CREATIVITY AND COOPERATION

Collaboration and cooperation are parts of many art processes, from musical ensembles, theatre productions, to class mural painting. Where does creativity lie in these sorts of endeavors? Does cooperation expand opportunities for individual creativity? Does individual creativity spawn creativity in peers? CRoC is beginning to sort through these questions in our creativity-focused program evaluation work.

We do know that in the two dozen cases where we have been asked to look in on creativity-focused programs, they all seem to in-volved students working in groups, either as a pervasive model or at key junctures throughout. We have also seen many instances where cooperative activity within a program is seen or reported to spill over into regular classroom or in-school behavior.

PART V.
CREATIVITY IN
THE WORKPLACE

WHAT BUSINESS AND POLITICAL LEADERS ARE SAYING ABOUT OUR NEEDS FOR A CREATIVE WORKFORCE. A LOT.

L et's revisit what our politicians and business leaders said above:

President Obama. *In a recent State of the Union address, President Obama suggested that education policies should "grant schools flexibility to teach with creativity and passion; to stop teaching to the test."*

IBM CEO Survey. *A recent international survey of 1500 corporate CEOs reported that creativity is now the most important* *leadership quality for success in business, outweighing even integrity and global thinking.*

Nissan CEO. *"Business begins with an idea. And as never before, its growth, stability, and ultimate success depend on innovation and a continuing flow of imaginative thought. The most urgent business of business is ideas.*

The voices of business and educational leaders, as well as our political leaders, urge creativity upon the nation. What they say and how they say it are revealing: about their underlying motivations, about their conceptions of creativity, about their expectations, about their sense of economic and social urgency concerning creativity, and of their frequent lack of thought about what can be done. We're bathed in a true cacophony, to mix metaphors.

This environment helped to spark the founding of CRoC in 2010 – we were motivated by confusion in the public discourse. It was time to help clarify the language surrounding creativity, assist with research in the field, and help draw together a national agenda (if one could be justified and imagined).

One piece of advice, when you hear that we need more creativity in the nation: ask the speaker or writer just how we should go about this.

We contend that it is not the 30 hour fifth grade workshop that is called for, though we are all for this as an ingredient. It will take a wholesale change in conceptions of teaching and learning to deflect America's pipeline to adulthood in the direction of creative development.

No individual or institution is positioned or empowered to direct such change; if it is going to happen, it begins with the individual teacher, the school science department, or the school principal bent on such an upgrade. We see these things happening in isolated instances, regionally across some schools such as groups of elementary schools in San Diego, but serious attention to creativity appears in no tangible national public policies. We may be tempted to think of the Common Core as an exception, but there is no indication that creative behavior and motivation will be assessed in tests linked to the Common Core.

CHAPTER 24

WHAT LEADERS ARE SAYING ABOUT HOW TO BOOST CREATIVITY. NOT MUCH.

I t's difficult to find prescriptions for large-scale practices that would address the expressed needs for a more creative workforce or more creative problem solvers generally. What kinds of action? And action by whom in the public or private spheres? Is there worthwhile practical guidance here?

At the present time, the loudest voice on needed change is the same loud voice that has directed school improvement and reform for at least 20 years: this is the voice of assessment and accountability – *establish assessments that measure the goals you espouse, and require schools one way or another to succeed on these assessments.*

We've worked under standards and assessment schemes for improving schools for a long time. Based on the *National Assessment of Educational Progress* results in periodic tests for 30 years, this does not work. We still have and 25 percent achievement gaps for low income and high-risk children, not to mention flat achievement across the board over these decades.

The emerging Common Core tests promise to require a different sort of thinking and performance among America's children. But the jury is out. If history is our guide, don't expect too much. We hope the cheerleaders for the Common Core are pointing to developments that can move the system toward more creative problem solving across the curriculum.

CHAPTER 25

WHAT ARE BUSINESSES DOING TO BOOST THE CREATIVITY OF THEIR EMPLOYEES?

There are indications that more and more product-focused businesses are giving more leeway to their research and development scientists to play with ideas. And with some visible results. We also see corporate and non-profit professional development efforts (such as on-site or retreat-type seminars) focused on creativity. We have our doubts about short-term general interventions. But a 2-day workshop on creative ways to handle customer complaints by phone is another thing – this could change behavior materially.[7]

---

7   As an aside, we are reminded of a scene from the Tom Peters film, *In Search of Customers.* The setting is a training session for FEDEX customer assistance agents who are learning how to keep *semi-irate* customers from reaching the *fully irate* stage. The tips

We also know that there are a great number of jobs where employers hope that employees will not exercise much or any creativity. The IRS auditor and Las Vegas blackjack dealer come to mind.

But when it comes down to most jobs, the ability to solve problems can benefit from some creative thinking. This goes for the order-taker in a fast food restaurant who has to deal with a disappointed and demanding customer as well as for the tire-changer at Firestone trying to free up a broken compressor. And when we dig in a bit, it applies to the auditor and casino dealer too – these jobs are not free of problems that these workers need to address effectively and creatively.

---

for getting such customers on your side probably work to minimize escalations in some cases – enough to warrant the training.

PART VI.
RELATED ESSAYS
AND REPORTS

THINKING ABOUT ASSESSING A CREATIVITY PROGRAM? WHAT ARE WE LEARNING THROUGH PILOT TRIALS AT CROC, AND WHERE CAN YOU GO FOR ASSESSMENT DESIGNS AND INSTRUMENTS?

This chapter draws from our evaluation work in 2014. Here we introduce our reasoning about how to set up evaluations, the nature of the scales we use, the use of the Next Generation Creativity Survey, and how we reach and report conclusions.

On the following pages, we show the executive summary of a report on five ArtScience related programs across the USA.

James S. Catterall

The Next Generation Creativity Assessment Project

Measuring Creative Behavior in the Arts, Sciences, and Social Problem Solving

Science and Art Laboratories
Bristol, Burbank, Orlando, Queens NY, Tustin CA

2014 Project Report

Executive Summary
September 2014

INTRODUCTION

This report describes the assessment of student creative development in five science and art laboratories conducted for high school students. The assessment was conducted by the Centers for Research on Creativity (CRoC).

The program launched in winter of 2013-14. Five sites were selected to host and administer the after-school program in Bristol, CT; Burbank, CA; Orlando, FL; Queens, NY; and Tustin, CA.

The Labs challenged secondary school students to explore issues and generate and develop innovative solutions to a wide range of problems within the context of the theme 'Energy of the Future.' Over the course of 4-5 months, mentors met with teams of students, once or twice a week, to identify problems, generate ideas/solutions, develop hypotheses to test, discuss, refine, and manifest their ideas. Students then presented their working models to a public audience and a panel of judges that selected a project from each site to compete at the international *Le Laboratoire* in Paris, France.

To obtain a longitudinal assessment of students' creative behavior and creative motivation at each Big Idea Labs site, CRoC used the *Next Generation Creativity Survey (NGCS)*. This survey instrument was developed and piloted by CRoC in six, diverse programs in 2012-2013.

During school year 2012-13, CRoC pilot-tested the survey in about 30 schools, including six programs in musical theatre, theatre, graphic design, a science/makers program, a youth leadership program, and an art/science laboratory.[8]

Self-reports and demonstrations of creativity. We measure creative growth in two domains using the *NGCS*. One domain is student views of their own creative behaviors and potential. This domain includes self-assessments of originality and fluency with creative ideas. Student self-reports also reflect student beliefs about their creative abilities, their skills and interests in collaborating, and their empathic orientations. Collaboration and empathy are widely valued dispositions in programs helping to boost children's creativity, as well as in learning situations more generally.

Actual creative products – today's creativity measurement. A recent trend in creativity research is based on the work of Harvard Business School Professor Teresa Amabile, who developed the Consensual Assessment Technique. This model advances the reasonable idea that actual creative products are good indicators of creative ability. In contrast, traditional tests, such as the *Torrance Test of Creative Thinking* skills, rely heavily on student reports of their own creative practices and not on actual products. We incorporated both techniques into the NGCS.

---

8 Participants were: Inner-City Arts in Los Angeles, The New York Hall of Science, Disney Musicals in Schools (New York and Nashville), and Playworks, Phoenix, AZ.

CRoC trains teachers and teaching artists to rate students' written ideas and drawings for creative content and aesthetic presentation.[9]

We compare scores from a pre-program administration of the survey to scores from a post-administration of the survey to produce what we call gain or growth measures.

Student self-reports of their creativity.

Our self-report measures include the following:

- Creative Motivation – eagerness to be creative; choosing creative actions
- Creative Problem Solving – approaching problems in creative ways; trying alternative solutions, experimenting, taking risks in making mistakes and errors
- Creative Self-efficacy Beliefs – believing one has high creative skills
- Originality – believing one generates novel or new ideas
- Collaboration Attitudes and Skills – enjoying collaboration; personal tendencies to be collaborative
- Creative Fluency – able to generate many ideas
- Empathy – understanding and responding to the feelings of others

---

9   Our raters are trained to a level of consistency required statistically for program level assessments of demonstrated skills and content – generally to within one point of each other on ratings and exhibiting no significant upward or downward bias in their ratings over time.

Demonstrated creativity growth.

We rate students' creative products on the *NGCS* in the following six areas:

- Demonstrated Creative Fluency: Generating more rather than fewer ideas
- Proportion (%) of Expressed Ideas Rated as Original. This item focused on student responses to our, "How would the world be different.....?" questions
- Ideas Rated as Valuable: Same item focus. Generating useful or aesthetic ideas to the "What if..." prompts
- Ideas Rated Original: Generating new or novel ideas across open items
- Drawing is Creative: Judges rating of student self-portrait
- Energy for the Future Topic is evident in writing and drawing. (Students tend to use Energy examples more on their post-surveys than on their pre-surveys.)

Next Generation Creativity Survey Results

Figure 2, Big Idea Labs, 2014: Growth in <u>Self-perceptions about own Creativity</u> Growth by Program Site and Scale							
			Demonstrated Creativity Scale				
Program Site	Creative Motivation	Creative Problem Solving	Creative Self-Efficacy	Creative Fluency	Originality	Collaboration	Empathy
Bristol	••••	••••••	••••••	••	•••••	•••••	
Burbank	•	••••••		••••	••••	••	
Orlando		••		••••			••
Queens					••		••
Tustin			•				
Standardized Gain Indications:	**Effect Size**						
.01 to .04	Trace	•	(Scale Gains are Adjusted				
.05 to .09	Small	••	For the Standard Deviations of Pre-Scores)				
.10 to .17	Modest	•••					
.18 to .25	Moderate	••••					
.26 to .29	Substantial	•••••					
.30 and higher	Strong	••••••	Centers for Research on Creativity, 2014				

How is growth in student creativity measured?

Our first way of gauging results on our survey is to calculate *average* gains in creativity scale scores for each of the five program sites.

Figure 2 displays these results. All sites implementing Labs in 2013-2014 reported some gains in average scores on student self-reports of their own creativity, from the pre- to the post-survey. These result from questions such as, "How easy is it to come up with lots of ideas?" (creative fluency) Or, "Do you think your ideas are more original than most?" (originality). If the average of scores on a pre-scale was, say, 2.8, and the average of scores on the corresponding post-scale was 3.1, then the gain of 0.3 ends up in our Figure 2 and Figure 3 charts. (We convert numerical gains to standardized gains to make different scales equivalent.)

As shown in Figure 2, Bristol topped all programs with gains in six of seven self-report scales -- this is unprecedented in our results from the *NGCS* over two years. Burbank students, on average, gained in five self-report scales, Orlando in three, Queens in two and Tustin in one. Scale gains noted by four stars or more (****) are statistically significant. Gains with fewer stars are "real" and based on the program student's scores, but not considered significant. Small numbers of students adversely affect statistical significance in three of these programs – Burbank (6), Orlando (12), and Queens NY (12).

Which self-reported creativity scales are most impacted? Three self-reported areas of creative behavior were most impacted by the program: *creative problem solving, creative fluency, and originality* scales each showed gains in three Lab sites– or in a majority of sites. These scales are at the very core of creative behavior, and very important goals of the Big Idea Labs.

How did DMIS Boost Actual Creative Products?
In addition to the student views shown above, we rated actual student work on survey tasks. CRoC staff judged written and drawn responses using a standard scoring guide. Figure 3 summarizes program impacts on average Demonstrated Creativity scales.

Program Site	Creative Fluency	% of "What if?" ideas original	Ideas Rated Valuable	Drawing and other open response ideas original	Drawing is Creative	Energy for Future Topic Embraced
Bristol	••••••		••••••	••		
Burbank	••••					
Orlando						••••••
Queens			••••••			•••••
Tustin	••••					••••••

Figure 3, Big Idea Labs, 2014: Demonstrated Growth by Program Site and Scale

Demonstrated Creativity Scale

Standardized Gain Indications:	Effect Size		
.01 to .04	Trace	•	(Scale Gains are Adjusted
.05 to .09	Small	••	For the Standard Deviations of Pre-Scores)
.10 to .17	Modest	•••	
.18 to .25	Moderate	••••	
.26 to .29	Substantial	•••••	
.30 and higher	Strong	••••••	Centers for Research on Creativity, 2014

Average scale gains. All of the five Lab sites in 2013-2014 produced gains in one or more measures of demonstrated creativity. Topping the list, Bristol showed gains in 3 of the 6 scales. These scales included creative fluency, ideas rated as valuable, and general originality. Queens and Tustin gained in 2 scales. Orlando and Burbank gained in one scale.

Here are illustrative student responses to the survey prompt, "How would life be different if all animals could speak English and Spanish?"

Animals would be able to fight and speak for themselves. Less animal abuse. You would totally know if you had mice in your house.

Animals would have jobs like people do (penguins in a suit with a little briefcase). Penguins would be presidents.

Areas of greatest impact. The most common areas of growth in demonstrated creativity was creative fluency (boosted in three programs) and ideas rated as valuable, showing a gain in two sites. Plus in three of the five sites, students incorporated the theme for this year, *Energy for the Future*, in their discussions and drawings on the post-survey. There was little mention of energy issues on the pre-surveys.

Program Success in Prompting Individual Student Creativity

The results we present above reflect growth in creativity scales as average scale scores, post- versus pre-program. In a given site, some scales gain and some do not, on average. We used this perspective in Figures 2 and 3 above.

Another way to characterize program success is to determine how many students (or what percentage of students) individually benefit from participating in the Labs. This is similar to a "batting average." Out of all program participants, how many get "hits," or in the case of Big Idea Labs, how many participants attain increases and in just which creativity scales?

We use this analysis to show program success rates in the NGCS' eleven creativity scales -- the percentages of students gaining between the pre- and post-survey on each scale.[10]

---

10 We calculated success rates as follows: We first excluded the students who registered the maximum possible score on each pre-scale. These students could not make gains on these scales. Then we used the percentage of students gaining from among the remaining students – i.e., the percentage gaining from among all students who could possibly gain.

Figure 4: "Batting Averages" across the entire Big Ideas program.

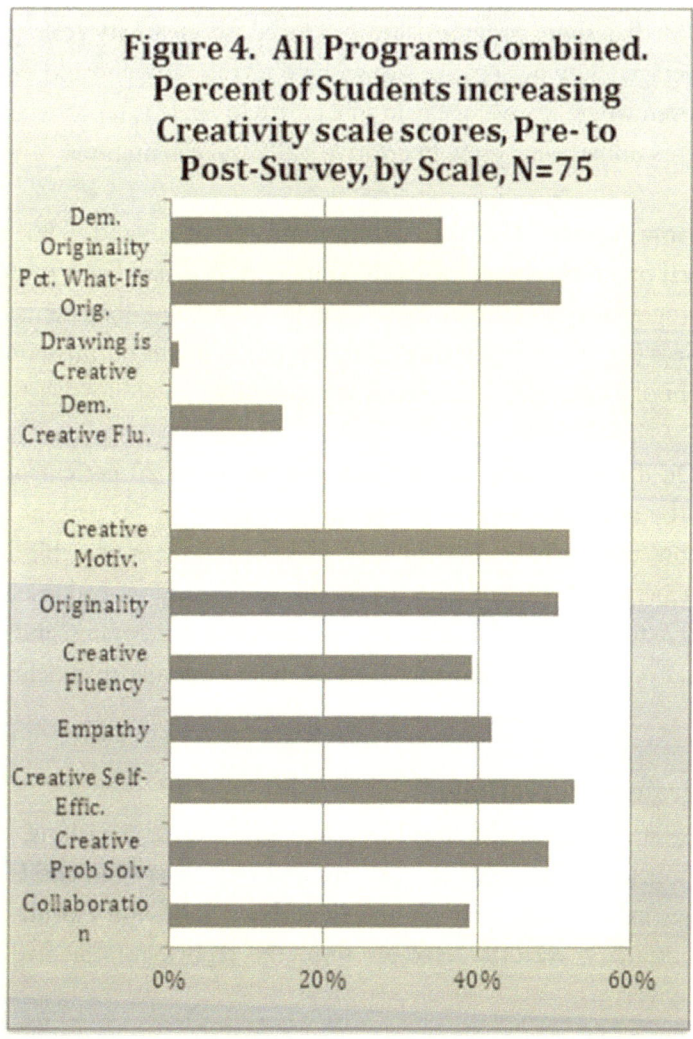

As shown in Figure 4, the five program sites together typically boost self-reported creativity scales (the bottom seven bars in the figure) for between 40 and 50 percent of their students.

These are important perspectives. Recalling Figures 2 and 3, we showed that some program sites produced no creativity scale gains, on average. The perspective shown here reveals, as we would expect, that even where no average gain in a creativity scale is reported, some students nonetheless grow in creative skills and orientations.

How important is this? An important goal of this and all learning-focused programs should be reaching more rather than fewer students. If a program boosts creative motivation for 50 percent of students in its first year (as we show in Figure 4), its aspiration might be impacting 60 percent of its students in subsequent years.

Or, if one program site shows a success rate of 20 percent on the empathy scale and another shows empathy gains for 50 percent of its students, there may be something worth knowing about why this difference emerged. We do caution that in this year's study, we had results for only 12 students in each of the Orlando and Queens programs, and these program differences in empathy gains are more suggestive than definitive.

Program Observations

CRoC staff visited each Big Idea Lab site on three occasions. Our Los Angeles staff traveled to east coast and west coast sites, and CRoC has researchers in place in Connecticut, New York, and Florida. For this summary, we offer excerpts from the report, for the five sites respectively.

The BRISTOL program appears to be exemplary in its execution, in the breadth and creativity of its energy-related ideas and products, and in the wide-ranging growth of student creativity on the NGCS creativity scales -- both self-reported and demonstrated.

We observed that the BURBANK Lab pursued the main model of collaborative, inventive, problem solving faithfully. They proceeded smoothly through effective phases of idea and product development. Students reported strong growth when indicating their own beliefs about their creative development.

The ORLANDO/EATONVILLE FL Labs were later getting started than others. They appeared to follow the ArtScience models of seeding ideas and problem solution design. The basic ingredients of idea generation and design were observed, the students enjoyed working with AS staff, and the mentors seemed cued to principles allowing students to work individually and collaboratively on their own ideas.

After starting out with a shortage of recruited students in December, the QUEENS N.Y. Lab rebounded to a successful program in the winter and spring. Although there were insufficient matched surveys to provide reliable NGCS survey results (in part because of program discontinuations by a dozen students), our observer recorded a well-functioning lab with earnest and productive students.

The TUSTIN Lab got off to an impressive, exciting start. They had solid initial enrollments and occupied a site that was undergoing some remodeling specifically to meet the needs of the lab. The mentors and staff were very excited about the program and about the site, and their enthusiasm seemed to rub-off on the students.

Conclusions and Implications.

Here are the main points we emphasize in conclusion:

1. Labs went from an idea in the minds of a few educators and organization leaders to an up-and-running set of five geographically dispersed programs in a matter of months. Considering the requirements – organizing training for newly appointed program managers/mentors, securing sites, planning schedules, planning local curricula, recruiting students and gaining permission from parents, rounding up materials for potential projects, scheduling presentations in non-school settings, recruiting judges, and planning travel for competition winners – this was quite a feat. On top of this, programs had to accommodate our survey processes and observations.

2. We expect program growth and a modest amount of operating "bug removal" if these Labs continue into future years.

3. Program mentors were for the most part exemplary in getting out of the way of kids to facilitate their origination of ideas and free up their choices of how to test their ideas. Labs were organized in ways that kept students attentive and engaged.

4. There was high satisfaction with the program among the many students who completed their projects.

5. There was high satisfaction on the part of mentors and other adults associated with the Labs. We did not follow the minority of students who left the program before finishing and don't know their reasons for leaving -- some students in this

category left within a short time after programs started. It was as if they had wandered into the wrong room at the start; or simply did not realize the degree of commitment and work the program entailed.

6. Most students worked in teams for their final projects and worked well as collaborators.

7. Students found formal presentations of their work challenging but doable. Only a few struggled, and struggle generally fell to the few teams that had not pushed their projects very far along. Students found the expert questions following their presentations challenging.

8. The Bristol, CT program showed very strong creative growth in both student self-reports and student demonstrations of their own creativity. And in the incidence of success with individual students in promoting aspects of creativity.

9. The NGCS survey results for the Bristol Labs creativity survey are so positive that they compel close scrutiny by program designers, educators, and others, as to how this program was organized and executed.

10. The Burbank site was very strong in its student reports of creative behaviors and dispositions.[11]

11. Growth of student "creative fluency" was strong in comparison to other measures across sites. Creative fluency refers to abilities to generate many ideas when called upon. This aligns with a major Big Idea Labs goal of "idea generation" by participating students.

---

11 Dispositions include inclinations, tendencies, and motivations to pursue what's measured in our scales. A creative behavior is something observed or claimed. Creative dispositions include motivation to behave creatively, creative orientation to problem solving, and seeking problems in the environment that warrant exploration.

12. Variations in creative gains across individual sites – Bristol, Burbank, Orlando, Queens, and Tustin – should interest administrators, educators, and artists who want to better understand the sources of these differences. I.E., keeping an ear tuned to what elements of Lab sites drive program success.

13. The labs should make efforts to fully enroll programs with well-informed students at the start. This would contribute to program success and also provide significant student populations for creative growth assessments within individual labs.

14. Full enrollments would give mentors consistent critical masses of students to work with and place all programs on a similar footing where any assessments are concerned.

15. A second year of operation would give researchers a chance to obtain more robust measures of student development. Combining this with a more intensive documentation of instructional practice could generate information helpful to individual labs. Additional inquiry strategies could include:

    • Systematic interviews and/or surveys with program mentors to document the Big Idea Labs experiences from adult and educator viewpoints.

    • Assessments of programs from the host clubs' perspectives

End of Executive Summary

CHAPTER 27

LOCATING CREATIVITY IN STEM AND STEAM PROGRAMS

We find that Science, Technology, Engineering, Arts and Mathematics programs (STEAM; or STEM) are promising places to engage creativity as a core part of an interdisciplinary curriculum. Perhaps surprisingly, our focus in this has been in the Engineering component of STEM programs, although the arts can make contributions to creative thinking across the curriculum. The following essay appeared in the inaugural issue of the *Steam Journal* (Claremont (CA) Graduate University, 2013).

The STEAM Journal
Volume 1
Issue 1 Luminare Article 6
March 2013

Getting Real about the E in STEAM

James Catterall

University of California - Los Angeles, California, USA

Abstract

STEM and STEAM are in the news. Researchers and educators in my field (cognition, art, and creativity) argue reasons for adding the A to STEM. While I visit this below, my focus is elsewhere. In this brief essay, I want to explore the meaning and importance of the E appearing in both STEM and STEAM. What's engineering doing in this mix? And what are some reasons for affirming the arts when the role of engineering is clarified?

Author/Artist Bio

Dr. James S. Catterall is Professor Emeritus and past Chair of the Faculty at the UCLA Graduate School of Education and Information Studies. Dr. Catterall is an Affiliate Faculty member at the UCLA Center for Culture, Brain, and Development. Dr. Catterall is also the Principal Investigator at the Centers for Research on Creativity, (CRoC), based in Los Angeles and London, UK. (www.croc-lab. org). Dr. Catterall is coauthor of "Critical Links: Learning in the Arts and Student Academic and Social Development," Arts Education Partnership's (AEP) 2002 landmark compilation, which provides summaries of numerous significant research studies in dance, drama, the multi-arts, music and visual arts as well as comprehensive summaries written by some of the most recognized names in arts research.

Getting Real about the E in STEAM
James S. Catterall

STEM and STEAM are in the news. Researchers and educators in my field (cognition, art, and creativity) argue reasons for adding the A to STEM. While I visit this below, my focus is elsewhere. In this brief essay, I want to explore the meaning and importance of the E appearing in both STEM and STEAM. What's engineering doing in this mix? And what are some reasons for affirming the arts when the role of engineering is clarified?

It can't be news to the readers of this journal that enhanced science, technology, engineering, and mathematics education, or STEM for short, is widely considered a path to a revitalized United States. Witness the geometric growth of STEM-related programs in the nation, and the reverence conferred on these programs by politicians and business leaders wanting to say something important and hopeful about American schools.

Norm Augustine, retired Lockheed CEO was exemplary in October 2012 when he called upon: "… industry and government to promote more STEM education in the U.S. 'Failure to do so… will undermine the U.S. economy, security and place as a world leader.' Competing with knowledge-based resources will be one way that the U.S. can recover and retain primacy in the global marketplace" (Twittweb, 2012).

A billboard for the Los Angeles Fund for Education glares out over Burbank, California: "Support Los Angeles Schools" in 8-inch letters, and in 8-foot letters "or FACE CATASTROPHE." A possible reference to technological obliteration?

More than a decade ago, state school boards and legislatures nationwide practically gave up suggesting or dictating changes in how schools taught in favor of testing students to be sure they were learning. Assessment and accountability trumped educational ideas. Education oversight became a matter of deciding what to test and how to reward and punish schools and districts based on student performance.

STEM is defying this cycle. STEM ideas have attracted a diverse and powerful crowd excited to see schools deliver when it comes to the sciences, mathematics, and technology. Once again, resources are concentrating on a cluster of learning objectives considered poorly served, goals that are perceived to succeed mainly in the education systems of our economic competitors.

The advent of STEAM. A revisionist delegation recently sidled up to STEM. Here were educators convinced that the Arts had a legitimate place in science and technology education. The point was NOT that you couldn't teach physics or mathematics without the arts, but that artistic expression and principles could assist learners in structuring and organizing ideas, exploring disciplinary and cross-disciplinary connections, and solving scientific problems. Furthermore, the STEAMers contended, creative practice in the arts might boost capacity and dispositions to think creatively in the sciences. A drawing or model of chemical bonds could be both practical and aesthetic -- and perhaps through its visual charm, all the more engaging to learners.

To some, STEM should be STEAM. While STEM programs haven't rushed to embrace the arts, a movement was born. RISD, the Rhode Island School of Design, quickly took a leading role in STEAM education leadership:

"STEM to STEAM is a RISD-led initiative to add Art and Design to the national agenda of STEM (Science, Technology, Engineering, Math) education and research in America. STEM + Art = STEAM. The goal is to foster the true innovation that comes with combining the mind of a scientist or technologist with that of an artist or designer.

RISD President John Maeda and other members of the community have been championing the idea that STEM expands into STEAM when art is part of the equation" (RISD, n.d.). And the advocacy group STEAM-not STEM has argued:

"Much research and data shows that activities like Arts, which use the right side of the brain, supports and fosters creativity, which is essential to innovation. Clearly the combination of superior STEM education combined with Arts education (STEAM) should provide us with the education system that offers us the best chance for regaining the innovation leadership essential to the new economy" (STEAM, n.d.).

Evidence supporting the A in STEAM. The cognitive research community has explored roles of the arts in science and mathematics learning in recent years, with positive results in individual studies investigating such things as music learning and spatial reasoning (Catterall & Rauscher, 2008). Neuroscientists, for example Professor Nina Kraus at Northwestern University's Auditory Neuroscience

Laboratory, are reporting a wide array of effects of music experience on neurobiology, brain function, and brain structure (Kraus, 2012). Based on accumulated individual studies, it is fair to say that we understand a great deal about how various visual and performing arts experiences impact diverse areas of understanding (Deasy, 2002).

The STEAM team has a substantial research-based case for the potential roles of the arts in science and technology learning. The practical challenge is devising instructional and curricular applications and ways to bring arts-infused science and mathematics learning to today's classrooms, and bringing the whole operation to a scale that could bring pervasive impacts to American science and industry. This is no easy prospect. The world of STEAM is beginning to sort these questions out.

What about the E? STEAM is a natural. Science, technology, engineering, arts, and mathematics education go hand in hand – there are elements of all five domains in each of them, at least some of the time. Science needs ever-better measurement instruments (technologies) to advance. The design and calibration of instruments require mathematics. And artistic ways of representing and understanding scientific concepts are commonly accepted, perhaps most widely by scientists themselves. When engineering is included as the practical application of science and technology to the creation of processes and devices, the cluster is complete.

But is it? The E for engineering takes on something of an outsider role in what STEM and STEAM actually mean. We teach science in the schools; we teach mathematics; and we teach the arts. We also use technologies in the schools and think about their connections to science and mathematics. Think of the wave tank in physics, the microscope, the analytical balance in chemistry, and even the chromatograph in biology. But engineering is not present in the school curriculum. Engineering is for later. Engineering is a college major, an applied science career bringing us better materials, processes, and products; or it is a means to land a Rover on Mars, organize flows of traffic, deliver drug therapies more effectively, and to solve myriad real-world problems in between.

The high school curriculum is a precursor to the practice of engineering. The original STEM movement surely included the E because science and mathematics training was a known foundation of engineering. If the impetus for STEM education was innovation and competitiveness in business, the largest portal to success is through our engineers. But "STM for E" lacks elegance as an acronym.

A and E. The Arts and Engineering. It would be nit-picking to fault the inventors of STEM for misapplying engineering on their banner. But the case described above provides good reason to give STEM and STEAM a little additional thought right now. It would be a good idea to clarify and reinforce the place of engineering in these initiatives. When schools or systems enact these programs, emphases gravitate to science, mathematics, and technology. We don't have high school engineering textbooks. We could say we don't have technology courses either, but technology is so pervasive in our lives and so integral to the worlds of science, that bringing technology to the core of STEM is seamless. Where engineering is concerned, the tacit assumption of STEM and STEAM seems to be that participating schools prepare students for successful careers in engineering. But students are not typically exposed explicitly in either STEM or STEAM initiatives to what engineering is about, with exceptions of course.

Design Education. Right here, the arts could reenter the discussion and help to bind STEAM into a coherent whole. Simply put, schools could elevate design education in the curriculum. Yes, pursuits in the visual and performing arts generally, and the integration of ideas from the arts into science and mathematics specifically, are important to STEAM. But design and engineering go hand in hand, and a basic course in design is developmentally and "curricular-ly" appropriate when it comes to a comprehensive STEAM-focused education.

Design begins by recognizing needs for processes and technologies, thinking, sketching and modifying ideas, organizing learning around what the task and design solutions require, revising, learning more, collaborating, and getting feedback. Design processes can relate science and technology understanding to what's being designed. Mental imagery and artistic 2D and 3D sketches and models – and of course CAD, computer assisted design, are core parts of designing.

The following comments suggest the flavor of learning in design:

"Every contrivance of man, every tool, every instrument, every utensil, every article designed for use, of each and every kind, evolved from very simple beginnings" Robert Collier. (Bizcommunity, n.d.)

"Having an idea in the first place is just the start; bringing that idea to life in a way that inspires others to help it grow can mean the difference between an abandoned sketch on a notepad and a successful finished product in a customer's hands" Lucy Blakemore.

If elementary and secondary students in STEAM programs were offered instruction, challenge, and opportunity in design, they may better understand, and personally integrate, science, mathematics and technology ideas in their views of the world and its problems. They might even aspire to engineering careers with a clearer sense of what they could contribute to society and to their own lives by doing so.

Just how design education could interface with STEAM programs is a design problem of serious magnitude, one that some programs are surely working on. Nonetheless, an overarching goal might be the cultivation of a design identity in STEAM education that propels how students learn and solve problems in the arts and sciences. The student as designer may go as far as any vision to realize what STEAM is all about.

References

Bizcommunity (n.d.). Bizcommunity.com. Daily Industry News. http://www.bizcommunity.com/Quotes/196/13.html

Catterall J. S. and Rauscher, F. (2008). Unpacking the impact of music on intelligence. In W. Gruhn (Ed.), *Neurosciences and music pedagogy* (pp. 171-202). Hauppage, NY: Nova Science Publishers.

Catterall, J. S. (2009). *Doing well and doing good by doing art: A 12-year longitudinal study of arts education – effects on the achievements and values of young adults.* Los Angeles, CA: I-Group Books.

Deasy, R. (Ed.). (2002). *Critical links: Learning in the arts and student academic and social development.* Washington DC: National Endowment for the Arts, The Arts Education Partnership.

Kraus, N. (2012). Biological impact of music and software-based auditory training. *Journal of Communication Disorders*, 45. 403 – 410. doi:dx.doi.org/10.1016/j.bbr.2011.03.031

Twittweb (2012). Ex-Lockheed chief: Invest in math and science education. http://twittweb.com/news+lockheed+chief+inv-26073489

RISD. (n.d.). STEM to STEAM. Rhode Island School of Design. http://www.risd.edu/About/STEM_to_ STEAM/STEAM (n.d.). Science, Technology, Engineering, Arts, and Math. http://steamnotstem.com/about/

A CONSUMMATE DESIGN PROFESSIONAL TAKES UP THE PROMISE OF DESIGN EDUCATION IN TURNING AROUND AMERICA'S LOW PERFORMING SCHOOLS.

ARTS TURNAROUND SCHOOLS:
The Design Challenge

James S. Catterall and Frank Gehry[12]

What if you read in these pages that reading achievement for American 13 year olds had rocketed up by two whole percentage points *in total* over the past 20 years; and that math proficiency since 1994 grew by less than 4 percent? If your math scores were decent, you would conclude that the nation had improved its schools by less than one quarter of a percentage point per year. In the case of some things that grow, like waistlines, you'd fail to notice change of this magnitude and be happy for it. In the case of education, there is little to celebrate.

---

12 James S. Catterall is Professor Emeritus at the UCLA Graduate School of Education and Information Studies and Director of the Centers for Research on Creativity, Los Angeles/London U.K. Frank Gehry, the world-renowned architect is Director of the Frank Gehry Foundation.

Continuing, you also notice that these paltry gains are not shared by everyone. In a long era when anyone and everyone involved in education improvement has focused on problems of the inner city, even this barely traceable improvement is not distributed equally. Low income children averaged only about half of the accumulated achievement growth of their more advantaged counterparts. Let's round this off to zero.

Well, guess what? You are reading these pronouncements and they are true. The *National Assessment of Educational Progress,* our most long-standing and reputable national yardstick of educational outcomes, has quietly reported these trends (well, flat lines) for about 30 years, most recently in volumes of *The Nation's Report Card,* through the Institute of Educational Sciences at the U.S Department of Education.

We point to this grim picture not to personally fault anyone in the system (others do plenty of this), but to underscore the fact that systematic education improvement on a large scale has proved elusive, even with declared Education Presidents and Governors leading the way. Of course we've seen wins and losses. But a nationwide problem deserves more than we've mustered, and deserves whole new approaches to change.

School Turnarounds are the latest in a long string of school improvement models, an idea that will have to move resolutely to avoid joining a dozen or more school reform initiatives that have been disowned and cast aside since 1960. The *President's Committee on the Arts and Humanities* is launching today a second and larger flight of experimental school overhaul programs called *Arts Turnaround Schools.*

Time will tell on the longevity and effects of Arts Turnarounds, but there is much to like in this initiative. Here's what we see:

- The visual and performing arts can be productive partners in language learning
- Music experiences have proven benefits for spatial reasoning, and in turn mathematics
- The arts engage children, and engagement in arts classes spills over into regular school activities
- The arts promote diverse ways of knowing
- The arts promote creative problem solving. And designs for solving problems
- The arts connect widely to diverse cultures
- The arts promote social and emotional development – including children's sense of agency and motivation
- Students highly involved in the arts are more likely to engage in pro-social behavior such as community volunteering
- The arts promote collaboration and empathy

An important overarching point is that learning in the visual and performing arts not only connects to the academic learning at the center of our school improvement structures. *The arts also cultivate more complete human beings who can accomplish and be much more than the content of their standardized test scores.* When did we last see the captain of a school reform project lead off a culminating speech with a claim that the students grew in empathy, or in their ability to work together? And when did we last hear an employer say that what they most sorely wish for in their young adult workforce is higher test scores?

Will Arts Turnaround Schools achieve all of these things from day one? No. What these schools face can best be described as a design challenge. They need to create and implement learning and social systems that revolve around what they are trying to achieve and that work in unprecedented ways. Perhaps the first homework assignment, for everyone in an Arts Turnaround School community should be, naturally, designing the school.

CHAPTER 29

ART, EMPATHY, AND CREATIVITY FROM BEHAVIORAL AND NEURO-IMAGING PERSPECTIVES

A Neuroscience of Art and Human Empathy: Aligning Behavioral and Brain Imaging Evidence

James S. Catterall
Professor Emeritus, University of California
Centers for Research on Creativity
jamesc@gseis.ucla.edu
www.croc-lab.org

Introduction

This chapter explores possible ties between rich participation or engagement in the visual and performing arts during adolescence and the cultivation of human empathy by early adulthood. We present behavioral evidence from a 12-year longitudinal study that supports the existence of such a relationship. And we articulate why these connections could be considered reasonable. In the second part of the analysis, we explore an arts-pro-social behavior link based on what we know of the neural substrates of artistic perception/expression and empathic behavior. Here we draw on one relatively young literature, the *neuroscience of art*, and on one relatively mature literature, the *neuroscience of human empathy*. Our methods of analyzing the common structures and mechanisms in these two bodies of literature must be considered speculative but potentially promising.

The principal sources of data are the National Educational Longitudinal Study of 1988 (NELS:88) which describes the arts experiences of youth over middle and high school as well as long term statuses through age 26, a meta-analysis by Jean Decity and Philip L. Jackson (2004) outlining the neural architecture of empathy, and a systematic review of recent studies exploring the neuroscience(s) of visual and performing arts experiences. The basic question explored is the degree to which artistic experiences and empathetic expression have common neuro-corrolates – thus lending support to a neurological argument for why the arts may promote pro-social behavior.

The Arts and Pro-social Behavior

We turn here to a large-scale study where students deeply engaged in the visual and performing arts during middle and high school reported significantly more pro-social or empathic behavior as young adults than comparison students who had few or no experiences with the arts. Thus a suggestion of the research is that learning and experiences in the arts helped promote capacities or dispositions for empathy.

Figure 1

Indicators of Involvement in the Arts Used in
***Doing Well and Doing Good by Doing Art* (Catterall, 2009: 38)**

Grade 8	Attends Concerts	Goes to art museums
	Attends art class 1x per week or more	Attends music 1x per week or more
	Attends drama 1x per week or more	In band or orchestra
	In chorus or choir	Participated in dance

Grade 10	In drama club	N courses in art
	N courses in music	N courses in drama
	In band or orchestra	In school play or musical
	How often takes music, art, or dance class	

Grade 12	Participated in school music group	
	Participated in school play or musical	
	How often takes music, art, dance class	

Note: In constructing involvement scale, extra point awarded for being an officer in an activity.

Distribution of Indicators: music (12), theatre (5), visual art (4), dance (3).

The differences were significant for low-income students, for high-socioeconomic status (high SES) students, and for the all-student samples. The most interesting analysis in this study derived from the low-income subsample, where students highly involved in the arts were compared with students lacking in arts involvement. The compared groups represented the top and bottom 12 percent on an arts-participation scale. This scale included taking arts-related classes in and out of school along with performing with in-school and out-of-school orchestras, ensembles, bands, dance groups, and theatre groups. Figure 1 shows the names of indicators of arts engagement drawn from the database to construct a scale.

Evidence on engagement in the arts and pro-social tendencies.

Pro-social, empathy-linked behaviors.   The pro-social behaviors shown in this 2009 study are widely linked to qualities labeled empathy in the literature.   For example, Roberts & Strayer (1996) found that individual empathy measures predicted various pro-social behaviors toward friend and peers for boys (ages 5-13), and pro-social behaviors toward friends for girls across the same ages.   By turning this around, these pro-social behaviors might be considered indicators of empathy.

Catterall's (2009) *Doing Well and Doing Good by Doing Art (2009)* speaks to the argument under construction here.   This study reports that intensive involvement in the arts during middle and high school associates with higher levels of subsequent educational achievement and college attainment, and also with diverse indications of pro-social behavior such as voluntarism and political participation. (We also note that a long history in psychological research characterizes empathy as a fundamental underpinning of pro-social behavior (Roberts & Strayer, 1996; McMahon, Wernsman, & Parnes, 2006). Merabian et al. (1988) note that individuals who possess high emotional empathy are more likely to be emotional, be altruistic in relations to others, volunteer to help others, be score higher on measures of moral judgment.)

In addition to individual measures of engagement in the arts, arts-rich high schools in the NELS study promote pro-social behavior in similar patterns.   And through investigating their instructional practices and organization structures, the researchers found that arts-rich schools bear characteristics that may account for their advantages, such as more cooperative learning environments, reading novels in the curriculum, and more teachers with positive job satisfaction.

In the realm we called doing good, the high-arts students were more active as community and youth volunteers across various groups, and both registered and voted more frequently. High-arts students are more than twice as likely as low-arts students to:

- Volunteer for a youth organization
- Volunteer for a civic or community organization.

In addition, high-arts students are about 15 percent more likely to register to vote, more than 30 percent more likely to have voted in the most recent presidential election, and about 20 percent more likely to have voted in any election in the 24 months leading to the last NELS survey panel.

There is additional important evidence in the work with the National Educational Longitudinal Survey of 1988. This is the observation that reported levels of community service among the key low-income group study grew substantially for some students between the ages of 14 and 16 but not for others (Catterall, 1997). A sizeable difference in this respect shows in Figure 2.

Figure 2

Community Service Involvement: Early vs. Late High School, Low SES students, percentages involved by age and by level of arts involvement.

	High Arts Involvement	Low Arts Involvement
	Performs some or more Community Service	*Performs some or more Community Service*
Age 14	24.50%	16.80%
Age 16	34.80%	14.00%

Catterall (1997) p. 7 and 8.

Figure 2 shows the percentages subjects performing at least some community service as of age 14 (spring of grade 8) and age 16 (spring of grade 10). When comparing the low-income students with high arts involvement to low income students generally lacking involvement in any art discipline, the contrast is substantial. High-arts students showed a substantial increase in community service activity over this period of schooling (a period in which they were highly engaged in arts). The growth amounts to an increase of 42% when the sum of activity is considered. The low-arts, low-income group actually saw decreases in community service activity over the same 2-year period. If any hypothesis of arts-effects on empathic behavior is to survive challenges, and if community service may be thought to have roots in human empathy, then the contrast shown in Figure 2 serves to support this sort of hypothesis.

By age 26, high-arts NELS participants scored significantly higher than low-arts students on measures of socially integrated activities (attending plays and concerts, participating in organized religion, frequenting libraries and reading books). High-arts students also showed more than twice as much community and youth volunteer service and a significant edge in voting registration and voting itself.

Where this leads us is to a contention that engagement in the arts promotes pro-social tendencies in youth. At least the sort of engagement assessed in the 2009 longitudinal study just cited. It is reasonable in any event to think that if particular circumstances promoted through arts engagement lead to circumstances shown in research to be formative when it comes to "doing good," there may be a link. And if there is such a link, that unusually high and sustained levels of arts-engagement might show more substantial and probable effects than would more casual or fleeting involvement.

Figure 3 shows differences in pro-social behaviors between arts-rich youth and arts-deprived youth assessed at age 26:

Figure 3

Indicators of Community Service Involvement: Age Low SES students, percentages involved by high vs. level of arts involvement.

	High Arts Involvement	Low Arts Involvement
Youth organization volunteer	24.3%	10.8%
Civic/community volunteer	24.6%	10.4%
Registered to vote	77.7%	67.1%
Voted, 19969 US Presidential Election	52.5%	35.1%

Catterall(2009) p.63,

Erratum: 1996 US Presidential Election

Empathic behavior

Human empathy is vital in social relations and in the maintenance of stable societies. Empathy can be considered a regulatory influence on certain behaviors – a force for compassion and helping behavior in the face of another's distress as well as a deterrent to destructive or harmful acts because of empathy for possible victims. Individual empathetic behavior has three or four components. One is *comprehending* the feelings of another individual – a fundamentally cognitive process. The second is the act of *feeling* the emotions of another, and a third is the capacity to distinguish self and others' feeling, and a fourth is inclination to act on behalf of the other's situation.

In general, research on empathy has focused on observed situations in which the other in question is in some type of pain, or is suffering the associations of negative situational conditions. Research has generally enlisted still images, typically photographs, of people in possibly empathy-inducing situations. Video or film images have been used, as have artistic visual representations depicting human facial expressions and situations.

Empathy goes beyond acts in the present; empathy also refers to individual assessments of prospective or imagined conditions. Thus anticipating the likely consequences of future conditions bearing on another individual take importance. A key outgrowth of this view is that individuals may regulate their own behavior related to others based on empathetic concerns for the consequences of their own actions. For example, not harming others in myriad possible ways because of not wishing to inflict pain or otherwise harm someone else. Empathy would not be considered the only determinant of harm/no-harm decisions; measured empathy in any circumstance has recognizable variance across individuals. But empathy associates significantly with expressed intentions and with actual behaviors in longitudinal studies. For example, individuals scoring higher on empathy scales exhibit lower levels of aggressive behaviors toward others (Jolliffe & Farrington, 2004).

From a behavioral standpoint, empathy is usually considered a trait – an individual disposition or inclination to recognize painful circumstances in others and to feel or resonate with feelings perceived in others. Empathy as a human trait is considered in the psychological literature to be developmental. A typical view is that very young children do not exhibit empathy, that empathic behavior emerges in childhood, and empathy grows more or less steadily until early adulthood (Grühn, Rebucal, Diehl, Lumle, & Labouvie-Vief, 2008) – more where conditions are conducive and less in some inhibiting climates. Many studies report declines in measured empathy beyond the mid 20s; but a careful review shows that there seem to be no systematic declines or increases in empathic tendencies beyond this age. Significant cohort effects on average empathy levels are reported. For example, consistent surveys over time show that today's college students exhibit considerably less empathic behavior than did college students 30 years ago (Zaki, 2011).

Research on the precursors of empathetic behavior stress qualities of home life of young children. One factor particularly stands out: this is the emotional stability and nurturing behavior of the child's mother. Indications are that children and adolescents whose mothers experienced high levels of family stress, family dissolution, single motherhood, and poverty associate display less empathy. Consistent, nurturing, and positive mothers' attention associates with the cultivation of empathy. (Zhou, et al., 2002). The use of corporal punishment in childhood and early adolescence associates with low empathy in youth (Lopez, Bonenberger, & Schneider, 2001). Another factor is the quality of social relationships with peers such as having good friendships and enjoyable interactions with schoolmates.

Empathy and pro-social behavior

There appears to be widespread agreement that engagement in pro-social behaviors is grounded in dispositions toward empathic actions. Decety and Jackson (2004) describe the connection occurring as early as age 18 months: "It is about the 2nd year that empathy may be manifested in pro-social behaviors (e.g. helping others, sharing, or comforting) indicative of concern for others (p.78)." McMahon,

Wernsman, and Parnes (2001) describe empathy as a predictor of pro-social behavior among African American adolescents. Strayer (1996) found ties between emotional expressiveness, indicators of empathy, and pro-social behavior. The list goes on.

The desire to help or comfort others may contribute to desires to volunteer on behalf of children or others with apparent needs. Volunteerism is a main component of "doing good" in the longitudinal analysis of behaviors associated with intensive involvement in the arts. We do not equate empathy and pro-social behaviors for important reasons. Empathy refers to understanding the feelings of others, feeling the emotions of others, and keeping track of whose feelings are whose. To some, empathy also involved some motivation to act on behalf those who we empathize with. Pro-social behaviors are just so: behaving on behalf of others or on behalf of a community. For now, we'll assume that pro-social behavior is more likely to occur in individuals more disposed to empathic reactions to others.

Why should the arts promote empathy?

Primary empathetic reactions occur when an observer sees or imagines another individual experiencing an emotion that the observer in turn understands and feels. There is of course a torrent of situations in daily life where this arrangement may arise. Empathy is typically a natural reaction to an observed situation where the observed is in pain, or requires assistance to meet an immediate need, or perhaps experiences great joy in present circumstance. It is also a natural response of anticipating the feelings or thoughts of others and the ability to connect to imagined situations and fictional characters.

The visual and performing arts involve representations of human circumstances that can convey much of what day to day experience brings – and often involving extremes of emotion -- with ample opportunity for observers, players, and the artists themselves to engage in self- and other- understandings. Empathetic capacity is active in both primary and secondary creating in the arts: primary being the construction of new works during which art making processes the artist is in empathetic connection with her audience: and secondary being the interpretive shaping of artworks for impact, such as performing a piece of music, during which time the artist must be in empathetic connection with both the primary creator of the work and the audience. Also, empathetic capacity is essential in both the artist's roles (primary and secondary) and the audience role of being able to make authentic connections with works made by others; good arts instruction includes development of all these roles.

In the **visual arts**, in the observer's role, paintings and sculptures often require appraisal of human faces and human figures for emotional signs and cues to help in their interpretations of what a work of art may be about, or to determine what's going on in its depiction. Or they engage the more subtle capacities in empathetically connecting to non-representational artworks by connecting to the gestalt of a piece, being able to read the symbolic and gestural human language. In the creator's role, students learning to paint and sculpt figures are as empathetically involved in depicting human emotion and affect through what they paint or carve as sophisticated artists are. In the arts classroom, the roles of creator and audience mix, as the capacity to make an authentic personal connection to something a student sees in a peers' artwork or in a masterwork lives immediately adjacent to the acts of construction. With greater artistic skill, empathy becomes subtler, enabling students to read features as subtle as brush-stroke traces bringing emotional tones to a painting, causing the artist to attend to such signals and the observer to incorporate such signals into understandings of figures or images in the work of art.

Music ties to emotion and empathy in the case of making music as well as simply in listening, again in the roles of creator (composer), performer, and audience. Playing music in ensembles requires complex empathetic skills, making ensemble rehearsal and performance as much a human community experience as a music experience. Musicians develop feeling and understanding for the emotions, as well as for the joys, needs, and predicaments we might say, of fellow musicians -- and for the feelings and understandings of themselves as performers – and additionally for the best ways to connect with their audiences. Making music is a fluid enterprise, requiring adaptations or modifications along the way, responding empathetically to many different kinds of cues in the real-time improvisation of performance. And it often becomes even more complex when working with a musical director whose "needs, "concerns, and interpretations require serious attention. All the while the musician is attending nearly autonomously responding to the sound as it goes forward – slipping in and out of grooves, adjusting volume or timbre, or just sitting out, based on an empathetic grasp on what is unfolding on these multiple levels in real time.

Listening to music unleashes a number of imagined human situations where empathy may be involved, some of which can be described in words, some of which are so subtle that the musical language is the only way to describe the shared experience of an emotion. This empathetic capacity in the language of music is often activated in the imagination, even when one cannot perform well musically, such as imagining you are a cellist, or *The Who*'s drummer, or singer Ertha Kitt, or maestro Gustavo Dudamel, this empathetic projection of self puts you in juxtaposition with another as sure as seeing a performer in concert does.

Dance is a consummate laboratory for empathic processing. This is because the dancer uses the body exclusively, along with facial expression, to express meaning, emotion, and mood, and we connect empathetically in the audience role, as well as in the primary and secondary creative roles. And we are varyingly equipped to "read" and understand the dancer through empathic responses to body orientations and movements. If seeing a human face provides emotional cues that can be empathically reflected in our own faces as we watch, empathic and mirroring responses involving the entire body may seem comparatively rich if not overwhelming. The choreographer's use of an original posture and relationship between two bodies can communicate a message that is impossible to understand outside of the empathetic language of movement. Dancing also evokes empathetic connection in audiences because we can feel the effort and the accomplishment of dancer's movements in our own bodies, so our bodies reach and leap along with the dancer's trained body as we connect to their message.

Dancing in ensembles or companies is, like music, a human community experience. Dancers develop feeling and understanding for the emotions, as well as for the situations of fellow dancers -- and for the feelings and understandings of themselves as performers. Dancers will play their feelings and emotions off of those of a partner, or of all dancers on stage, the space between them becomes eloquent to those who can feel it -- understanding themselves, attempting to understand others; acting without words.

Theatre and drama offer a quintessential platform for engaging empathic dispositions. It is often said that theater is the art form that most resembles life as people live it, and so it invites an immediacy of empathy that bypasses some of the uncertainties about disciplinary artifice that those less familiar with the arts sometimes feel. The actor must develop a sense of a character to initiate a role – understanding that character in a sociocultural context. More than this, the actor must grow to understand other characters in a production – empathizing in turn to put the action on a footing suited to who the players intend to be. And the actor must be in real-time empathetic connection with an audience in order to be effective. Similarly, as audience, people must be able to "willingly suspend disbelief" in order to connect with the characters in a play.

It should be noted that the abiding reason these different roles in these four disciplines tend to develop empathy is that it feels good. It is satisfying to draw and have ones ideas seen and recognized. It is rewarding to know the audience is feeling exactly what you intended during the musical phrase. It is personally meaningful to sense an audience moving with your dancer's reach. It is humanizing to feel what a character feels in a well-wrought play. Whereas any act of empathy rewards with some kind of positive reinforcement, the connections made through artistic media are particularly rewarding to us. This may well explain why the four main arts disciplines appear so early in humankind's history, beating the wheel by tens of thousands of years, and have only had the literary and media arts added since the Pleistocene Era.

From a behavioral standpoint, there appear to be reasonable arguments embedded in the discussion above suggesting that engaging in the visual and performing arts put participants into situations where self- and other- understandings are a helpful if not a seamless part of the process. We thus reach an argument that the arts may "promote" pro-social behaviors because of their intertwinement with empathy-laden relations and opportunities. That the arts embrace empathetic communication is underscored in Leslie Brother's discussion titled "A Biological Perspective on Empathy" in which he states (quoting Schafer 1959), "…empathy requires 'attention … to cues … in motility, verbalization, affective expression, and tempo." It would be difficult to compress a testimony to art and empathy into a shorter statement. Affective expression is central to music, acting, dance, as well as figural and scenic painting. Tempo and motility more generally bring emotion to musical expression, linguistic phrasing, communication through movement and dance, and communication through cues of rhythm and motion in the visual arts. Our facial expressions and bodies signal emotions and feelings. And so do our words. We empathize because of what we see, feel, and mirror in another or in another's symbols. But the human voice carries emotion as well as feeling that may mix with other signals prompting empathic response. And actors, after all, have lines to feel, embody, and speak, and literal, social, and cultural understandings to achieve on stage. It is quite possible that humans have developed no media more exquisitely suited to the development of empathetic capacity than the arts, which argues for their early emergence and profound durability. The arts have provided an essential species survival advantage of enabling us to empathetically connect and succeed together.

A neuroscience view

Up to this point, we have done the following. There is evidence that high levels of involvement in the arts while in school associate with (and perhaps promote) pro-social behavior in young adulthood.

There is good reason to believe that pro-social behaviors are rooted in capacity and motivation for empathy. And we've argued that, on the surface of things, it appears that both doing and observing in the visual and performing arts may be well suited to the exercise of empathy.

We turn here to a brain-based interpretation of these connections. We begin with a summary treatment of the neuro-architecture of empathy. What fundamental brain processes are involved in empathic responses to situations and cues? And then we turn to neuroscience of art. The same question: what fundamental brain processes are involved in experiencing or doing art? The purpose of these questions is simple: if the arts engage neural processing in ways similar to, or overlapping with, empathic responding, perhaps engagement in the arts associates with subsequent pro-social behavior because the arts promote the capacity of the brain for empathy.

The underpinnings of the hypothesis are these. High levels of activities that prompt empathic assessments or promote empathic understanding may be seen as causing activations in requisite neural circuits. Basic ideas of neuroplasticity suggest that such exercise should strengthen the circuits involved. The pathways would thus find empathic understanding (and empathic assessment) "easier" or more fluidly processed. The neurons fire more dynamically; the requisite dendritic and axonal networks become more robust and reach targets more efficiently. We note that in a situation of neural process enhancement, we should expect the advent of efficiencies over time, not *more* lighting up of involved areas in a brain map, but *less*. But relative activation is not the question here – we're interested in whether or not the arts might promote efficiency in empathy response because the arts may act to enhance empathy-involved pathways. And whether increased dispositions for empathy result.

The Data

Our goal is to compare the neural substrates of art and empathy. Our main approach to this comparison was to explore the neuroscience literature related to art and to empathy for any consensus about the neural circuits activated in each.

We first searched and assembled what we refer to as our core references in the neuroscience, neuro-function, and neuroanatomy of empathy. These core resources are labeled in as such in the references to this paper. We found substantial commonality across these (and eventually other) studies in describing the neural architecture of human empathy. The common areas of activation included: the prefrontal cortex, the dorsolateral prefrontal cortex, the temporal parietal junction, and the anterior cingulate cortex. The limbic system joins in these activations. (We do not pursue details of limbic system activations for this analysis, at this time anyway.)

Figure 4 on the following page points out the tasks, responsibilities, or functions of these cortical areas, as described across our core literature.

Figure 4

Cerebral processing related to empathy

Prefrontal Cortex, Premotorcortex (and mirror neurons)
- Attention to human voices
- Processing emotional stimuli
- Processing self-reflections
- Attribution of intention to others
- Joint attention
- Emotions, important connections to ACG

Dorsolateral prefrontal cortex
- Adopting perspective of another (with TPJ)
- Infer intentions of other
- Self assessment

Temporoparietal junction
- Social perception and empathy
- Emotions vs self-reflections in decision-making
- Response to visual motion
- Gesture imitation
- Music performance processing
- Performing creative tasks

Anterior cingulate gyrus (and mirror neurons)
- Self-other overlap during social perception (mirror neurons)
- Visuospatial attention
- Processing of emotional cues

PFC:	Pre-frontal cortex; 8,9,10,46 (Brodmann)
DL-PFC:	Dorso-lateral prefrontal cortex; 9,46
TPJ:	Temporal-parietal junction (Inferior parietal/superior temporal; 10,39,22
ACG:	Anterior cingulate cortex; 24,33,34

The main tasks within empathetic behavior are to attend to others and self, adopt the perspective of others, and infer the intent of others (*theory of mind*), and distinguish the emotions of other and self – all central processes in empathic behavior. The six brain regions listed below are the most frequent sites of brain activation identified in studies of empathy:

- pre-frontal cortex
- dorsolateral prefrontal cortex,
- temporoparietal junction (and the inferior parietal/superior temporal regions),
- anterior cingulate gyrus
- premotor cortex,
- mirror neurons (concentrated in the PFC and to lesser extent in ACG)

Studies related to brain region activations during empathic thinking/ feeling include the following. This figure is extended on the following page with indications of which specific brain regions show activation in each study.

**Figure 5: Neural Substrates Described in studies of the visual and performing arts;
Neural substrates of Empathy, Reading, and Mathematics from Meta-analyses**

VISUAL ART	*aesthetics*	Cela-Conde, C.J., G. Marty, F. Maestú, T. Ortiz, and E. Munar, et al. "Activation of the prefrontal cortex in the human visual aesthetic perception." Cinzia, D.D., and G. Vittorio. "Neuroaesthetics: a review." Current Opinion in Neurobiology 19, no. 6 (2009): 682-687.
	aesthetics	Cupchik, G.C., O. Vartanian, A. Crawley, and D.J. Mikulis. "Viewing artworks: contributions of cognitive control and perceptual facilitation to aesthetic experience." Brain and Cognition 70, no. 1 (2009): 84-91.
	aesthetics	Di Dio, C., E. Macaluso, and G. Rizzolatti. "The golden beauty: brain response to classical and renaissance sculptures." PLoS ONE 2, no. 11 (2007): e1201.
	aesthetics	Jacobsen, T., R.I. Schubotz, L. Hofel, and D.V. Cramon. "Brain correlates of aesthetic judgment of beauty." Neuroimage 29, no. 1 (2006): 276-285.
	aesthetics	Kawabata, H., and S. Zeki. "Neural correlates of beauty." *J. Neurophysiology* 91, (2004): 1699-1705.
	aesthetics	Mendez, M. "Dementia as a window to the neurology of art." *Medical Hypotheses* 63, no. 1 (2004): 1-7.
	aesthetics	Vartanian, O., and V. Goel. "Neuroanatomical correlates of aesthetic preference for paintings." Neuroreport 15, no. 5 (2004): 893-897.
MUSIC	*emotion*	Koelsch, S., T. Fritz, D.Y. von Cramon, K. Müller and A.D. Friederici. "Investigating emotion with music: an fMRI study." Human Brain Mapping 27, no. 3 (2006): 239-250.
	emotion	Kreutz, G., and M. Lotze. "Neuroscience of music and emotion." In W. Gruhn and F. Rauscher (Eds.), Neurosciences in music pedagogy, New York: Nova (2008): 143-168.
	emotion	Overy, K., and I. Molnar-Szakacs. "Being together in time: musical experience and the mirror neuron system." Music Perception 26, no. 5 (2009): 489-504.
	emotion	Overy, K., and I. Molnar-Szakacs. "Music and mirror neurons: from motion to 'e'motion." Social Cognitive and Affective Neuroscience 1, no. 3 (2006): 235-241.
	perception	Koelsch, S., and W.A. Siebel. "Towards a neural basis of music perception." *Trends in Cognitive Sciences* 9, no. 12 (2005): 578-584.
	pleasure	Blood, A.J., and R.J. Zatorre. "Intensely pleasurable responses to music correlate with activity in brain regions implicated in reward and emotion." Proceedings of the National Academy of Sciences of the USA 98, no. 20 (2001): 11818-11823.
DANCE	*empathy*	Berrol, C. F. "Neuroscience meets dance/movement therapy: Mirror neurons, the therapeutic process and empathy." The Arts in Psychotherapy 33, (2006): 302-315.
	skill-acquisition	Calvo-Merino, B., D.E. Glaser, J. Grèzes, R.E. Passingham, and P. Haggard. "Action observation and acquired motor skills: an FMRI study with expert dancers." Cerebral observation and acquired motor skills: an FMRI study with expert dancers." Cerebra Cortex 15, no. 8 (2005): 1243-1249.
MOVE-MENT	*empathy*	Gallese, V., and D. Freedberg. "Motion, emotion and empathy in esthetic experience." *Trends in Cognitive Sciences 11, no. 5 (2007): 197-203.*
	perception	Vaina, L.M., J. Solomon, S. Chowdhury, P. Sinha, and J.W. Belliveau. "Functional neuroanatomy of biological motion perception in humans." Proceedings of the National Academy of Sciences of the USA 98, no. 20 (2001): 11656-11661.
ACTING	*empathy*	Blair, R. "Cognitive Neuroscience and Acting: Imagination, Conceptual Blending, and Empathy." The Drama Review 53, no. 4 (2009): 93-103.
CORE EMPATHY		
CORE READING		
CORE MATHEMATICS		
		See the following page for legend and discussion of CORE studies.

Immediately below the shaded bar in Figure 5 appear our entries for what we refer to as the core neural substrates for empathy. The bold omegas (Ω) serve as markers for brain regions or areas identified with, in this first case, the main empathic processes observed in neuroscience research. The six regions identified above are marked.

(Legend: MNS mirror neuron system; PFC prefrontal cortex; DL-PFC dorsolateral PFC, PMC premotor cortex; ACG anterior cingulate gyrus; TPJ temporopareital junction; SupT superior temporal lobe; InfP inferior parietal lobe; OFG orbital frontal gyrus; PAR parietal lobe; TEMP temporal lobe; OPFG orbital prefrontal cortex; OCC occipital lobe; DOM hemispheric dominance, Left or Right.) Figure 5 (cont'd):

James S. Catterall

MNS	PFC	DL-PFC	PMC	ACG	TPJ	SupT/InfP	OFG		PAR	TEMP	OPFC	OCC	DOM
	Ω	Ω											
	Ω												
	Ω		Ω		Ω								R
	Ω					Ω							
	Ω			Ω									
	Ω	Ω		Ω	Ω	Ω	Ω						R
			Ω	Ω									
Ω	Ω												
	Ω												
Ω	Ω												
Ω			Ω										
	Ω				Ω								
	Ω	Ω		Ω					Ω				
Ω	Ω												
Ω	Ω												R
Ω													
Ω	Ω	Ω	Ω	Ω		Ω							R
									Ω	Ω		Ω	L
									Ω		Ω		L
MNS	PFC	DL-PFC	PMC	ACG	TPJ	SupT/InfP	OFG		PAR	TEMP	OPFC	OCC	DOM

A final column signals any left or right hemispheric dominance (more realistically, a "tendency toward dominance" in the literature, here showing right hemispheric "leaning" in the case of empathy).

Our characterizations of the neural substrates of art are not collapsed in Table 5 for purposes of this analysis. For one reason, we did not locate any analysis or meta-analysis of the neuroscience of art, one that could help paint the broad sort of picture that emerges with neuroscience studies of empathy. For another reason, the arts are widely distributed across behavior and cognitive modes. And without the benefit of some meta analysis we were not sure that we would expect the artistic behaviors of acting, viewing painted images, singing, playing jazz, or dancing a wolf would show common activations and circuits in the human brain.

We instead searched the cognitive neuroscience literature for neuroscience studies exploring artistic expression and interpretation. Our search concentrated on the period 2000-2010. This is not an expansive literature, but it is growing. In spring 2010, we identified 19 such studies, with a median publication date of 2006-2007. Seven of these studies addressed visual art, six addressed music listening or playing, five explored dance or music, and one addressed acting.

For each study, we identified the neural substrates of the behavior identified by the author(s). Visual art behaviors are dominated by studies probing aesthetic judgment (e.g. work probing what happens when a subject believes a painting is beautiful or not). Where these paintings involved figural representations, empathic processing may be related to such judgments. Five of the six music studies expressly focused on emotion – the sixth on music perception. Two of the music studies focused on the mirror neuron system (MNS), which is intimately tied to processes of other and self-understanding, emotion, and feeling. One of the two dance studies probed mirror neuron function. The acting study was an essay by a neuroscience academic that did not address neural substrates.

We undertook our scan for arts-related neuroscience research without an intention to capture or stress studies that related to emotion or empathy. The search assistants had no such instruction. But as described just above, what we turned up did show high levels of cross-over activations and neural circuitry between the arts and empathy.

Brain regions activated through the arts show a concentrations in the areas noted for Core Empathy Activations. Thirteen of 18 arts studies show activations in the pre-frontal cortex. Six studies involve the anterior cingulate gyrus. And five studies show activations in the temporoparietal junction or superior temporal/inferior parietal areas.

A global picture emerges that can be described this way. Neuroscience studies in the visual and performing arts show modest to considerable involvement of the brain areas and regions known to process empathic responses and behavior.

This global assessment takes on added meaning, and possibly importance, when we consider two more elements. – core activations revealed in studies of learning to read and in studies of mathematics processing. We include these because the object of first interest in this study was the long-term comparison of students highly involved in the arts versus students not involved in the arts during their last five years of secondary school. Among other occupations during these school years are the concentrated pursuits of language and reading development and mathematics understanding. Since these subjects probably engaged our high-arts students as much or more than their artistic pursuits, it's worth having a look at the core neural substrates of reading and math.

What shows is a stark contrast to the neural correlates of empathy and the arts. Reading shows mainly in the main inferior areas of the brain: the temporal, parietal, and occipital lobules. Mathematics instantiates in the parietal lobule and orbital-prefrontal cortex.[13]

We include a crude map of these results as Figure 6. This shows a lateral medial view of the human brain and shows indications of the primary activation areas for emotion and the arts (common areas in this rendering), reading, and mathematics. There are three principal messages in Figure 6. Emotion and the arts have a lot in common, a concentration of these overlaps is in the prefrontal cortex, and reading and math processing have little traffic with the areas of the brain mapped to emotion and art.

---

13 We must point out that the involvement of anterior regions of the brain with reading, such as we have described, are linked with *learning* to read – letter sounds, phonemic awareness, and decoding words. We do not make claims about advanced reading behaviors such as reading novels, historical texts, or textbooks. In mature reading, there are obvious situations where concern for others may be important, if not mainly the concern of what is read. This a gap of unknown dimensions in our argument to the extent that we do not bring evidence to bear on behavioral connections between advanced reading and the possible advancement of empathetic skills and dispositions.

Figure 6

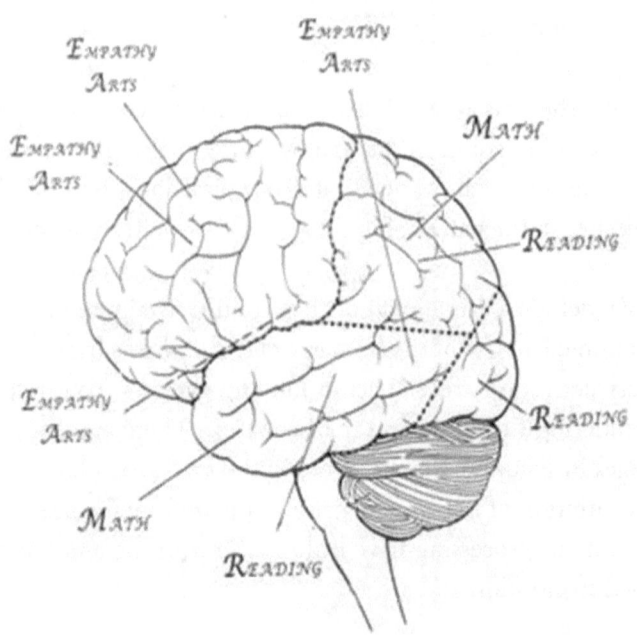

Discussion

The purpose of this analysis was to investigate neuronal structures and processes that might help account for behavioral observations indicating that youth with comparatively high levels of engagement in the arts while in school develop comparatively high rates of pro-social behavior as young adults. These observations came from a 12-year longitudinal study of 12,000 students; as such, the relationship should be considered more grounded than any deriving from the sort of short-term, small study-population research that characterizes much of developmental psychology.

Our hypothesis began with a conjecture that pro-social behaviors – for examples volunteering on behalf of youth or others in the community and political participation – can build on individual empathic dispositions. We found support for this in the literature discussed above. We also proposed that the visual and performing arts engage human symbolism, communication, and empathetic understanding at their very centers, in both pronounced and subtle ways.

Our hypothesis grew then to our main question of interest. Since the arts, pro-social behavior, and empathy seem behaviorally enmeshed, do the neural substrates of empathy and the neural substrates of art have significant elements in common? As with many topics in neuroscience, the primary evidence indicating that particular areas or regions of the brain serve particular purposes comes from various imaging techniques – many in the mainline neuroscience journals from functional magnetic resonance imaging, or fMRI. This technique literally lights up areas of the brain as research subjects carry out specific tasks. Having an empathic reaction to a depicted situation or assessing a painting for aesthetic qualities are two such tasks that have been subjected to such imaging studies.

Most of what we worked with were studies that pointed to one of several dozen specific brain areas as the center(s) of activity, or sometimes more crudely to global regions such as the main lobules of the brain. Ultimately, as we showed in Figure 5, our analysis came down to consensus views of where empathic processing, or where artistic experiences turned on these lights. The resulting views are generally, although not exclusively static. The closest our views came to describing neural circuitry in action was the pathway, demonstrated convincingly by Jean Decety, between the dorsolateral prefrontal cortex and the temporoparietal junction when imaging empathic behavior. Our descriptions miss other neural circuits that could be considered important but perhaps peripheral to the main neural stories of empathy and art – communications with the limbic system, with the amygdala, and with the insula particularly did not rise to the surface in our literature scans. But we achieved a visually satisfying representation of unambiguous commonalities between art and empathy. And by a rough calculus, these commonalities steer well clear of core functions involved with learning to read and basic mathematics processing, two leading preoccupations during the school hours.

So at a very crude level, it appears that neural processes involved with art in fact have a potential to develop a capacity for empathy and pro-social behavior. This suggestion rests on neuroplasticity: intensive and repeated activities in the arts may associate with pro-social behavior because they condition empathy-related architectures in the brain.

Future research? Our analysis points to additional studies that might inform its suggestions. Assuming the outlines of neural processes described above are at least plausible, a central argument that may deserve additional testing is that experience can enhance empathetic behavior, and particularly that artistic experiences might boost dispositions toward empathy. In the best of designs, such studies would be longitudinal. A general approach would be to test empathetic responses in a group beginning artistic training – for instance learners about to concentrate in acting or figurative visual art (drawing, painting, or sculpture). Tests would include behavioral demonstrations of empathy and imaging for the neural substrates of empathetic cognition. Then after meaningful experience and skill development in the subject's artistic training (say 2-3 years of sustained work), we would test empathetic responses again, through both behavioral assessments and imaging studies. Would subjects be more likely at the follow-up to empathize with given stimuli? Would response growth, if any, vary by qualitatively different stimuli? Would brain activation (location of activity using FMRI and sequencing of activity using EEG-MEG imaging) differ from pre-assessment to post-assessment for a given stimulus?

We are not aware of analogous imaging studies in the arts or empathy literatures, nor analogue studies in the dynamics of brain plasticity that would help us reason through and refine designs for future studies. Readers are invited to point us in helpful directions.

References and Resources

Neuroscience studies in the visual and performing arts

Berrol, C. F. "Neuroscience meets dance/movement therapy: Mirror neurons, the therapeutic process and empathy." *The Arts in Psychotherapy* 33, (2006): 302–315.

Blair, R. "Cognitive Neuroscience and Acting: Imagination, Conceptual Blending, and Empathy." *The Drama Review* 53, no. 4 (2009): 93-103.

Blood, A.J., and R.J. Zatorre. "Intensely pleasurable responses to music correlate with activity in brain regions implicated in reward and emotion." *Proceedings of the National Academy of Sciences of the USA* 98, no. 20 (2001): 11818–11823.

Calvo-Merino, B., D.E. Glaser, J. Grèzes, R.E. Passingham, and P. Haggard. "Action observation and acquired motor skills: an FMRI study with expert dancers." *Cerebral Cortex* 15, no. 8 (2005): 1243–1249.

Calvo-Merino, B., C. Jola, D.E. Glaser, and P. Haggard. "Towards a sensorimotor aesthetics of performing art." *Consciousness and Cognition* 17, (2008): 911-922.

Cela-Conde, C.J., G. Marty, F. Maestú, T. Ortiz, and E. Munar, et al. "Activation of the prefrontal cortex in the human visual aesthetic perception." *Proceedings of the National Academy of Sciences of the USA* 101, no. 16 (2004): 6321-6325.

Cinzia, D.D., and G. Vittorio. "Neuroaesthetics: a review." *Current Opinion in Neurobiology* 19, no. 6 (2009): 682-687.

Cupchik, G.C., O. Vartanian, A. Crawley, and D.J. Mikulis. "Viewing artworks: contributions of cognitive control and perceptual facilitation to aesthetic experience." *Brain and Cognition* 70, no. 1 (2009): 84-91.

Di Dio, C., E. Macaluso, and G. Rizzolatti. "The golden beauty: brain response to classical and renaissance sculptures." *PLoS ONE* 2, no. 11 (2007): e1201.

Gallese, V., and D. Freedberg. "Motion, emotion and empathy in esthetic experience." *Trends in Cognitive Sciences* 11, no. 5 (2007): 197–203.

Jacobsen, T., R.I. Schubots, L. Hofel, and D.V. Cramon. "Brain correlates of aesthetic judgment of beauty." *Neuroimage* 29, no. 1 (2006): 276-285.

Kawabata, H., and S. Zeki. "Neural correlates of beauty." *J Neurophysiology* 91, (2004): 1699-1705.

Koelsch, S., T. Fritz, D.Y. von Cramon, K. Muller and A.D. Friederici. "Investigating emotion with music: an fMRI study." *Human Brain Mapping* 27, no. 3 (2006): 239–250.

Koelsch, S., and W.A. Siebel. "Towards a neural basis of music perception." *Trends in Cognitive Sciences* 9, no. 12 (2005): 578–584.

Kreutz, G., and M. Lotze. "Neuroscience of music and emotion." In W. Gruhn and F. Rauscher (Eds.), *Neurosciences in music pedagogy* (2008): 143-168. New York: Nova.

Mendez, M. "Dementia as a window to the neurology of art." *Medical Hypotheses* 63, no. 1(2004): 1–7.

Overy, K., and I. Molnar-Szakacs. "Being together in time: musical experience and the mirror neuron system." *Music Perception* 26, no. 5 (2009): 489–504.

Overy, K., and I. Molnar-Szakacs. "Music and mirror neurons: from motion to 'e'motion." *Social Cognitive and Affective Neuroscience* 1, no. 3 (2006): 235–241.

Vaina, L.M., J. Solomon, S. Chowdhury, P. Sinha, and J.W. Belliveau. "Functional neuroanatomy of biological motion perception in humans." *Proceedings of the National Academy of Sciences of the USA* 98, no. 20 (2001): 11656–11661.

Vartanian, O., and V. Goel. "Neuroanatomical correlates of aesthetic preference for paintings." *Neuroreport* 15, no. 5 (2004): 893-897.

Vartanian, O., and V. Goel. "Emotion Pathways in the Brain Mediate Aesthetic Preference." *Bulletin of Psychology and the arts* 5, no. 1 (2004): 37-42.

Neuroscience studies of empathy

Brothers, L. "A biological perspective on empathy." *American Journal of Psychiatry* 146, (1989): 10–19.

Carr, L., M. Iacoboni, M.C., Dubeau, J.C. Mazziotta, and G.L. Lenzi. "Neural mechanisms of empathy in humans: A relay from neural systems for imitation to limbic areas." *Proceedings of National Academy of Sciences USA* 100, no. 9 (2003): 5497–5502.

Decety, J., and P.L. Jackson. "A social-neuroscience perspective on empathy." *Current Directions in Psychological Science* 15, no. 2 (2006): 54–58.

Decety, J., and P.L. Jackson. "The functional architecture of human empathy." *Behavioral and Cognitive Neuroscience Reviews* 3, no. 2 (2004): 71-100.

Decety, J., P.L. Jackson, A.N. Meltzoff, and E. Brunet. "Empathy examined through the neural mechanisms involved in imagining how I feel versus how you feel pain."*Neuropsychologia* 44, no. 5 (2006): 752-761.

Decety, J., P.L. Jackson, and A.N. Meltzoff. "How do we perceive the pain of others? A window into the neural processes involved in empathy." *Neuroimage* 24, no. 3 (2005): 771-779.

Decety, J. and Lamm, C, The Role of the Right Temporoparietal Junction in Social Interaction: How Low-Level Computational Processes Contribute to Meta-Cognition. *NEUROSCIENTIST* 13(6): 580–593, 2007.

Eslinger, P.J. "Neurological and neuropsychological bases of empathy." *European Neurology* 39, (1998): 193-199.

Iyer A, Lindner A, Kagan I, Andersen RA. Motor preparatory activity in posterior parietal cortex is modulated by subjective absolute value. *PLoS* Biol. 2010 Aug 3;8(8).

Jimura, K., S. Konishi, T. Asari, and Y. Miyashita. "Temporal pole activity during understanding other persons' mental states correlates with neuroticism trait." *Brain Research* 1328, (2010): 104-112.

Lamm, C., C.D. Batson, and J. Decety. "The neural substrate of human empathy: effects of perspective-taking and cognitive appraisal." *J. Cognitive Neuroscience* 19, no. 1 (2007): 42–58.

Mathur, V.A., T. Harada, T. Lipke, and J.Y. Chiao. "Neural basis of extraordinary empathy and altruistic motivation." *Neuroimage* 51, no. 4 (2010): 1468-1475.

McMahon, S, Wernsman, J., and Parnes, A. L. Understanding Prosocial Behavior: The impact of empathy and gender among African American adolescents. *Journal of Adolescent Health* (39)1, 135-137, July 2006.

Seitz, R.J., J. Nickel, and N.P. Azari. "Functional modularity of the medial prefrontal cortex: involvement in human empathy." *Neuropsychology* 20, no. 6 (2006): 743-751.

Shamay-Tsoory, S.G., R. Tomer, B.D. Berger, and J. Aharon-Peretz. "Characterization of empathy deficits following prefrontal brain damage: the role of the right ventromedial prefrontal cortex." *Journal of Cognitive Neuroscience* 15, no. 3 (2003): 324–337.

Singer, T., B. Seymour, J.P. O'Doherty, K.E. Stephan, R.J. Dolan, and C.D. Frith. "Empathic neural responses are modulated by the perceived fairness of others." *Nature* 439, (2006): 466–469.

Singer, T., and F. de Vignemont. "The empathic brain: how, when, and why?" *Trends in Cognitive Sciences* 10, no. 10 (2006): 435-441.

Strayer, J. Empathy, emotional expressiveness, and prosocial behavior. Child Development (67) 449-470, 1996.

Neuroscience studies and reviews of mathematics

Ansari, D. Numeracy and arithmetic in the brain: the roles of development and individual differences. *Proceedings: Cognitive neuroscience meets mathematics education.* Brugge, Hot van Vatervliet, March 25-28, 2009.

...... Various contributors. *Proceedings: Cognitive neuroscience meets mathematics education.* Brugge, Hot van Vatervliet, March 25-28, 2009.

Holloway, I. D., Price, G.D., and Ansari, D. Common and segregated neural pathways for the processing of symbolic and non-symbolic magnitude: an fMRI study. *Neuroimage* (49)1, 1006-1017.

Neuroscience studies of reading.

Poldrack, R. A. and Sandak, R. (2004). Scientific studies of reading (8/3). Special Issue: *The Cognitive Neuroscience of Reading.*

Longitudinal, behavioral study of art and pro-social behavior
Catterall, J. S. *Doing Well and Doing Good by Doing Art: A 12-year Longitudinal Study of the Achievements and Values of Young Adults.* Los Angeles, CA: I-Group Books, 2009.

Centers for Research on Creativity

Los Angeles/London U.K.

Index

www.ingramcontent.com/pod-product-compliance
Lightning Source LLC
Chambersburg PA
CBHW030448290526
45786CB00001B/501